"If you truly want to become a better person, understanding *why* you do what you do is a key to changing *what* you do and *how* you do it. True transformation starts in the heart. Your 'heart' is the Bible's term for the center of your motivations. Jesus explained in Matthew 15:19 that the source of all that's broken, incomplete, and wrong in our lives is found in our hearts. Jeremiah adds that the problem is our hearts are deceptive (Jeremiah 17:9). We lie to ourselves more than we lie to anyone else— and that refusal to face the truth about ourselves causes problems in our relationship to both God and others.

Only God knows us completely as we really are. This is why we need God's perspective to understand ourselves. Other tools can teach us a lot about ourselves, but our understanding will always be incomplete without the perfect insights from God's Word.

That's why I'm excited about this new book by Matt Brown. Laying a solid biblical foundation of scriptural insight, my friend Matt shows why devout Christians have used the Enneagram for centuries as a tool to grow in Christlike discipleship. For ages, saints have used this simple construct to help themselves and others understand how God has uniquely shaped each of us for a special purpose *and* the pitfalls that accompany every strength. This book is going to help you a lot!

At the beginning of his famous theological masterpiece *The Institutes of the Christian Religion*, John Calvin wrote these words: 'Nearly all the wisdom we possess, that is to say, true and sound wisdom, consists of two parts: the knowledge of God and the knowledge of ourselves.' Calvin went on to explain that we can't really know ourselves without knowing God, and we can't really know the fullness of God without knowing ourselves This book will help you with both tasks."

—RICK WARREN

AUTHOR OF *THE PURPOSE DRIVEN LIFE*

"There are two great days in everyone's lives: the day they were born—and the day they figure out why. Never dull and always honest, Matt has written more than a book. *A Book Called YOU* is a call to live out a life of purpose and passion! You and your world may never be the same."

—RAY JOHNSTON
FOUNDING PASTOR OF BAYSIDE CHURCH
IN GRANITE BAY, CALIFORNIA

"It's the number one reason people fail to continue as global missionaries: they can't relate to others. God wants to open the eyes of the nations to the gospel, but first He has to open the eyes of the person closest to you—YOU!

Over the last decade, I've seen Pastor Matt Brown and his wife, Tammy, live out an authentic vision for the Christian life and transform our church by using both a biblical lens and tools like the Enneagram in order to help people heal, grow, and serve. I can now take all of my staff through years of teaching material because it's found in Matt's new book *A Book Called YOU*. I've seen God use this message to reveal blind spots and break unhealthy sin patterns holding people back from the lives they were called by God to live.

Just as James called us to look at ourselves intently and embrace what God shows us, we all need a mirror. I believe *A Book Called YOU* is a mirror God has given the church to help us see ourselves through the lens of gospel truth so that He might bring peace to our hearts and joy to the world."

—CLAUDE HICKMAN
EXECUTIVE DIRECTOR OF THE TRAVELING TEAM AND AUTHOR
OF *LIVE LIFE ON PURPOSE, IT'S ALL BACKWARD,* AND *REBEL*

a
book
called

YOU

a book called

YOU

**Understanding
the ENNEAGRAM
from a Grace- Filled,
Biblical Perspective**

MATTHEW STEPHEN BROWN

W PUBLISHING GROUP

AN IMPRINT OF THOMAS NELSON

Published in Nashville, Tennessee, by W Publishing, an imprint of Thomas Nelson.

Thomas Nelson titles may be purchased in bulk for educational, business, fund-raising, or sales promotional use. For information, please email SpecialMarkets@ThomasNelson.com.

Library of Congress Control Number: 2021942821

ISBN 978-0-7852-4085-3 (softcover)
ISBN 978-0-7852-4086-0 (eBook)

Printed in the United States of America

21 22 23 24 25 LSC 10 9 8 7 6 5 4 3 2 1

To Tammy, my amazing wife, who allowed God to bring
healing to our marriage by using the Enneagram.
To my three wonderful kids, Madison, Kennedy, and Ethan.
Thank you for loving a growing Three on the Enneagram!
To Sandals Church, which has followed me as I have
learned to be a pastor. And to Lori Zimbardi. This book
is a testament to who you are and the talent you have.

CONTENTS

FOREWORD

I love pastors Matt and Tammy Brown. Our paths crossed nearly a decade ago, and my life is richer for the relationship. I was so excited when I heard Matt was writing this book because they have lived these principles before their friends and congregation in times of hope and in seasons of pain. After reading the words of the manuscript aloud to my husband and one of my sons, I stayed up until after 3:00 a.m. reading more on my own. I love books that challenge and equip me to live holy and holistically. I believe it will do the same for you. In light of this, I want to revisit the words of David,

> I praise you, for I am fearfully and wonderfully made.
> Wonderful are your works;
>> my soul knows it very well.
>> **Psalm 139:14** ESV

Somehow David was able to ponder the wonder of himself and perceive the wonder of the God Most High. He referred to himself as *fearfully and wonderfully made*; it was a deep knowing he carried in his soul. When did we lose this wonder? We live in a day when people are more likely to describe themselves as confused souls who are *fearful and forever wondering*. But let's make this personal because, after all, this is a book about you. When was the last time you looked at yourself and thought, *Wow, I'm a wonderful work of God*? I'm not talking about arrogance and conceit. Our world is filled with that. I am talking about awe. Like what you experience when a baby is born into this world and the moment is pregnant with the purity and promise of what might be.

David would have understood the importance of this book. As we read on, we discover that this psalmist king is the one who penned that God had a book about you.

> Your eyes saw my unformed substance;
> > in your book were written, every one of them,
> > > the days that were formed for me,
> > > > when as yet there was none of them.

Psalm 139:16 ESV

I fear it is impossible to experience this type of wonder when you do not know that you are intimately known and uniquely loved.

I vividly remember when a portion of this wonder broke over me. Riveting insights will do that to you. I was weary after a trip to South Korea. As I laid on my bed, I could feel my body sinking into sleep. I was just about to enter a dream when I was jolted awake by a holy whisper.

I do not love My children equally.

What was this crazy thought that just crossed my mind? Was this concept blasphemous? Taken aback, I challenged the thought out loud.

"Father, You have to love us all the same, or it wouldn't be fair."

In reply, I heard these words:

I don't. Equal implies My love can be measured, and I assure you . . . it cannot. Same would mean My children are replaceable or interchangeable, and they are not.

I knew it was the Spirit speaking, but I felt so conflicted. Then I heard this phrase that revolutionized my understanding of the way God looks at each of us.

I do not love My children equally . . . I love them uniquely.

Take a deep breath and receive this. You, my friend, are uniquely loved.

God doesn't have love for you . . . He is love.

Even with all our failures and flaws, the flawless One calls you irreplaceable.

Saint Augustine said it best: "God loves each of us as if there were only one of us."

And it is true; there is only one of you.

Just to make sure I haven't lost you, let me share this example with you. If you are the parent of more than one child, you probably already understand this. When that second, third, or later child was born, your love was not divided. It was multiplied in ways that were immeasurable. There is no way you could quantify the love you have for each child. Your love for each child is unique. Your heavenly Father's love is no different.

We are uniquely loved because we are uniquely created. This book is not an attempt to label or limit you by a number. These pages will not give you excuses or make false promises. Each page lends insights designed to release you so you can know the truth. We all know that no one can do "you" better than you. And yet this reality does not negate the fact that all of us can find ways to do our "you" better.

And to do "you" better counterintuitively involves each of us becoming more like Jesus. This book marries Scripture and the Enneagram as tools to help you do just that. Each chapter is woven with personal stories and relational wisdom as well as examples from historical figures and heroes of the faith from the Word of God.

This concept of you as unique highlights one of the many reasons behind *A Book Called YOU*.

It wasn't written to put us into nine boxes; it was written to explain what hinders us from growing in community and relationship. There are reasons behind those unreasonable responses. You know the very ones that make you question yourself or others. We need to know the *why* before we can live out the *how*.

We all face challenges from very different places, which means we have stories that others need to hear and strengths that others lack. All of this treasury is at risk of being lost if we don't learn to interact respectfully and graciously with one another. Read and believe, because this book has the means to create pathways to move us forward in the right direction.

—**Lisa Bevere**
New York Times bestselling author

INTRODUCTION

Why You?

In one of the most famous Christian books ever written, *The Purpose Driven Life*, Rick Warren opens the first chapter with these words: "It's not about you."[1] No, it's all about God. So good, so true. But here is a question that comes to my mind next: *What is God all about?* The answer is YOU!

For years as a Christian pastor, I struggled to reach people for Jesus. I was on a mission. The problem was, I forgot that God was also on a mission—to reach me. And He is on a mission to reach you too!

I don't know how you feel about yourself. There are probably some things you like, some things you hate, and some things you've never told anyone about. We are all a mixture of self-confidence and insecurity. I am a person who leans toward insecurity (when you read the chapter about my personality type—Enneagram Three: the Achiever—you will understand some of the reasons why).

After I became a devoted Christian in college, I still struggled with way too many issues. I loved God, and I was born again. But I felt really stuck. I was saved but still a sinner. I was found but still incredibly lost. There were things in my life I was deeply ashamed of. There were things I felt I just couldn't share. I was deeply embarrassed and ashamed.

One of the most embarrassing things about me was my toenails. I know—not super spiritual but true. I was a soccer player all the way through college, and my feet were gross. Even when I got married, my wife loved me but hated my toenails. Isn't that somehow true for all of us? I mean, in the way that we may love someone more than anything, but if we're honest, there are probably things about that other person that are . . . well, just gross.

I would only wear sandals around people I trusted. In Southern California, where I lived, it seemed like everybody started wearing sandals in the nineties. Maybe people wore them before, but for me, I was pretty sure only Jesus wore them. I would only wear them around people I was really comfortable with. Even my closest relatives looked at my feet and were like, *"Gross!"* But I knew they still loved me, thank goodness.

I realized that if I ever started a church, it would be a place where people could see the very worst in me and still love me. Just as my wife loves me. Just as Jesus does. As I prayed about it, God laid on my heart the need to start a church that would be a place where people could be real, a place where they could talk about anything and everything and still be loved. A place for people to be real with themselves, with others, and with God. So I walked in obedience, and in 1997, I planted Sandals Church in Riverside, California.

When I started Sandals, I did almost everything wrong! (One day I want to write a book called *How Not to Plant a Church*! But let's see how this one does first.) I did everything wrong until I found something that helped me get it right. The early problems our church experienced were due to people not being real, despite our vison and all my best efforts. So the church and I floundered. Until I discovered the Enneagram. It helped change the way I see myself, the way I see others and, most important, how I see God in the way the Bible had always wanted me to see Him.

One thing I want you to understand as we get started is this: Jesus is the Surgeon, and the Enneagram is just a tool. When you have surgery, you don't thank the knife—you thank the Surgeon. God used the Enneagram to cut deeply and remove so much I didn't need. It has helped transform my life and the lives of thousands of people whom I am blessed to minister to.

The word *Enneagram* combines two Greek words: *ennea*, the number nine, and *gram*, which means "written," like a telegram or Instagram. It is simply a tool that helps us understand personalities and remixes the way we approach our relationships with God and others.

Many Christians have problems with the Enneagram because it's not in the Bible. I want to remind you that the finest Scripture scholars in the world were in Jerusalem when Jesus was born in Bethlehem. The Jewish leaders had Scripture, but Eastern, pagan "wise men" used nonbiblical methods to follow a star in the sky to find Jesus before the Scripture scholars found Him.

No one really knows where the Enneagram comes from. I personally think it's a little Christian and a little Eastern. I think some people who use the Enneagram are solid, and some are just plain weird. Some people are biblically grounded, and others are absolutely heretical. There is a lot of confusion about where it came from, but I have tons of clarity on what it can do for you. Here's why the Enneagram is so helpful: it doesn't just tell you what you tend to do; it helps you identify *why* you do what you do. The Enneagram gets at motivation. It helps you uncover the why.

I want you to find Jesus. Jesus wants you to find yourself. Jesus isn't lost or confused about who He is, but you might be. The Enneagram is the best tool I've ever found to begin the process of being real with yourself so you can be real with God and others. Understanding the Enneagram has helped me understand my wife. It's helped me understand my kids. It's helped me understand other people. And most of all, it has helped me understand myself.

I believe it is going to have a powerful impact on your life as well.

Some of you might like your spouse again after reading this book. You might find grace to change how you view that person at work you've been judging instead of loving. You might have sympathy for people who are raising their kids a little bit differently from how you raise yours. Understanding how God designed you and the people around you will help give you a grace-filled, biblical perspective on yourself, your spouse, your kids, and everyone else you do life with.

Everything we're going to discuss in this book is grounded in the Bible. We're going to look at the Enneagram, along with biblical principles, as a way for God to begin teaching you about yourself. Not all of us have the same strengths, and not all of us have the same weaknesses. We're all sinners, but we sin in very different ways. That's one of the reasons the Enneagram is a helpful tool.

The Enneagram describes nine basic personality styles that God designed. You are not a number; you are a uniquely created individual. However, the Enneagram numbers (or types) will help you better understand who you are and what drives you. Before I discovered the Enneagram, I was constantly frustrated with so many aspects of my personality. God used the Enneagram to show me my core sin and my core strength—and my life has never been the same.

In each chapter, we will get to know each type's general characteristics by observing someone in the Bible who exemplified that personality. Then we will dive deeper to uncover the core motivation and sin, study helpful passages of Scripture, learn how to love someone with that personality—and most of all, if you have that Enneagram type, discover how to be real with yourself, others, and God. Of course, you may not identify with every characteristic of your primary Enneagram style, or you may be a mix of two or three styles. That's okay! The descriptions in this book are for your general reference to help you understand the basic tendencies of people who identify with that personality.

Now, if you grew up religious or have been a Christian for a while, you might be a little uncomfortable with the idea of an entire book about *you*. You've been taught that the most important thing is to learn about God and to obey His commands. That is absolutely true. Most of us think we know the commandments, and we think we know what God has taught us to do, but we never include ourselves in that process.

So why should you read *A Book Called YOU*? Because knowing yourself is a commandment. In fact, Jesus included it in the greatest commandment.

The Greatest Commandment Includes *You*

Matthew 22:34 says, "When the Pharisees heard that Jesus had silenced the Sadducees, they gathered together" (NASB). In Jesus' day, the Pharisees and Sadducees were the two major Jewish political parties. So in today's terms, it would be like a religious leader shutting up both Democrats and Republicans. Neither Jewish political party knew what to do with Jesus.

The Sadducees had just asked Jesus a question about the resurrection, and His answer shut them up. So now it was the Pharisees' turn. They thought, *This guy may have shut up the Sadducees, but now we're going to test Him.* They found one of the smartest, brightest Pharisees, an expert in religious law, and they huddled together to trap Jesus by asking Him this question: "Teacher, which is the most important commandment in the law of Moses?" (v. 36).

Now, if someone asked you to summarize the entire Bible—all the books, all the writings, all the Scriptures—in one verse, could you do it? Jesus didn't even blink. He knew exactly what the most important commandment was. "Jesus replied, 'You must love the LORD your God with all your heart, all your soul, and all your mind. This is the first and greatest commandment'" (vv. 37–38). That was an acceptable answer. He hadn't offended anybody or shocked anybody with that.

But what Jesus said next changed the way Jews saw religion forever. This was radical. After Jesus described the first and greatest commandment, He said, "A second is equally important: 'Love your neighbor as yourself'" (v. 39).

Now, a lot of people see the word *neighbor* and think, *I need to be nicer to people. I need to be kinder. I need to be gentler. I need to be better to others.* I think most of us understand that. But the word they miss is *yourself.*

In the most important commandment, Jesus included *you.* You and I need to learn to love ourselves. We need to learn to care about ourselves, because if we don't know how to treat who we are, then how on earth are we going to treat our neighbors? How on earth are we going to know how to relate to God? Later in the Bible, Paul reinforced this important truth when he wrote, "The whole law can be summed up in this one command: 'Love your neighbor as yourself'" (Galatians 5:14).

Christianity Is a Relational Movement

Why is Jesus so interested in you loving God, you loving others, and you loving yourself? Because Christianity is a relational movement. And it's a relational movement in three directions: upward toward God, outward toward our neighbors, and inward toward our souls.

A lot of us think of Christianity as a religion, and the Christian life does have religious practices. But the reason we practice our religion is to connect with God relationally. It's the same reason my wife and I religiously practice date night—so we can connect relationally. If you don't give a relationship time, you don't have a relationship. The purpose of religious practices is to connect relationally. It's why we do what we do.

Christianity is a relational movement toward God, others, and self. First, we need *a right relationship with God*. Because of sin, we all have a broken relationship with God. That's why Jesus Christ came: because we were separated from God by sin.

Second, we need a *right relationship with others*. Sin not only tripped us up with our relationship with God, but it also messed up our relationship with each other. If you have kids, you've seen this work out, right? Your kids are going to fight with each other. They're not going to be kind to each other because sin tears apart relationships—even the most intimate bonds of a brother and a sister. Even within the context of the human relationships in which we should be the most loving and the kindest, we see sin working. It separates, and it divides.

Finally, we need *a right relationship with ourselves*. Not only does sin negatively affect our relationship with God and with each other, but it also affects my relationship with myself. Sin skews the way that I see myself. It blinds me to the real me. I don't see and understand myself.

Here's the problem: If you don't know yourself, how on earth are you going to know God? How are you going to relate to others?

A lot of people have a problem with being real with themselves in the context of Christianity. They understand they need to be real with God and go deep into Bible study. And they understand they need to be real with others and share the gospel. But they never think about being real with themselves. Guess what? Your relationship with God is limited by you! And in your relationships with others—guess what the limiting factor is? It's you!

If you want to experience everything God has for you, you first have to deal with yourself. You have to be willing to look inside and say, "God, who am I? What is it that I don't see about myself that You see?" We need to talk about you, and why we need to grow you, challenge you, and let God redeem you—and ultimately re-create you, once again, to become who He always meant you to be.

When It All Went Wrong

A lot of us don't realize why we are broken because we don't understand this concept called sin. So I want to take you way back. Let's go back before Jesus ever came to the earth. And let's talk about when it all went wrong.

Genesis 3 is a strange story. If you are new to Christianity, put your seat belt on and hold on, because we have a talking snake. And a lot of strange things happen, like naked people in a garden. It's all in the Bible. You have to read it! It's better than soap operas or reality TV, because one is totally fake and the other is an edited version of real. The Bible is all real, all the time, and it invites you to see people at their very best and worst moments. Genesis 3 may not show the lowest point of humankind, but it shows where it all went wrong. Genesis 3:1 states, "The serpent was the shrewdest of all the wild animals the LORD God had made. One day he asked the woman, 'Did God really say you must not eat the fruit from any of the trees in the garden?'"

In Genesis, God gave only one command: *"Don't eat of this tree. You can eat from anywhere else, but don't touch this tree."* Why? It was a special tree. It grew the fruit of the knowledge of good and evil.

"'Of course we may eat fruit from the trees in the garden,' the woman replied. 'It's only the fruit from the tree in the middle of the garden that we are not allowed to eat.' God said, 'You must not eat it or even touch it; if you do, you will die'" (vv. 2–3).

Most people don't understand what happened in Genesis 1–2. Let me just set the scene for you. God made the earth perfect for human beings. God created a garden, an orchard. It was a protected place for Adam and Eve to thrive, to do everything they wanted to do. God made it very clear: *"I love you. I've placed you here. Everything's beautiful; everything's wonderful."* But for Adam and Eve to be free beings meant there had to be choice. And so there was an option for evil.

That's what came up in Genesis 3:4–5. "'You won't die!' the

serpent replied to the woman. 'God knows that your eyes will be opened as soon as you eat it, and you will be like God, knowing both good and evil.'"

Adam and Eve were perfect, but they were naive. They didn't understand everything good, and they didn't understand everything evil, but they did understand obedience. They knew they weren't supposed to touch that tree. They knew it was wrong, but they willfully chose to disobey God.

That choice to disobey God is called sin. And that's why all our lives are broken—because God has said, *"Do things this way,"* and we've chosen our own way. Every time we do that, it breaks our relationship with God, it breaks our relationship with each other, and it breaks our relationship with ourselves. Sin is an equal-opportunity destroyer. Sin doesn't care who you are; whether you're rich or poor, young or old, sin will destroy your life.

Genesis 3:6 says, "The woman was convinced. She saw that the tree was beautiful and its fruit looked delicious." Now, we don't know what kind of fruit it was. It probably wasn't an apple—that idea came about five hundred years ago when some artists depicted it that way. The Bible doesn't tell us what it was; it was just a piece of fruit.

The story continues: "She wanted the wisdom it would give her. So she took some of the fruit and ate it. Then she gave some to her husband, who was with her, and he ate it, too" (v. 6). Where was Adam? Being a dummy, standing right there, sinning entirely along with Eve. She gave it to him, and he ate it. The Bible says, "At that moment their eyes were opened" (v. 7).

You see, part of what the Devil said was true. When you sin, you are going to be changed. You are going to know something you didn't know before. And the most dangerous lie is always the lie with a little truth mixed in.

The Bible says when their eyes were opened, for the first time as human beings, "they suddenly felt shame at their nakedness" (v. 7). Until this point, Adam and Eve didn't know they were naked. We've seen that before, right? All of us have probably been around a toddler. They don't care if they're naked; they have no concept of shame or awkwardness. To them, life is a naked party all the time. And then at about three years old, things change. (Hopefully, that happened to you, because if you're thirty and you're naked, that's weird, and maybe you need to be arrested.) For most of us at some point in our lives, we realize we shouldn't be naked everywhere. We feel ashamed of our nakedness. That's what we see in Genesis 3:7. For the first time in history, they realize, *Something is wrong with me.*

What did Adam and Eve do when they realized they were naked? "They sewed fig leaves together to cover themselves" (v. 7). That's the problem. That's why we struggle in our relationship with God. That's why we struggle in our relationship with each other, even in the context of marriage. We cover ourselves.

We're not real, we're not honest, and we're not truthful—and here's why: at the core of who we are, sin has made us all ashamed. We're not willing to be completely real because we're afraid and think, *If you really knew who I am, you wouldn't love me.*

I have good news for you! I don't know what you've done or where you've been or what's happened in your life, but God loves you. He loves you, and He doesn't want to cover you with a fig leaf. He wants to cover you with the blood of Jesus Christ that was shed for you on the cross.

The story in Genesis 3 goes on to say, "When the cool evening breezes were blowing, the man and his wife heard the Lord God walking about in the garden" (v. 8). What was God doing? Remember, Christianity is a relational movement. God was walking, and He was moving toward a relationship with Adam and Eve.

How did Adam and Eve respond? "They hid from the LORD God among the trees" (v. 8). Adam and Eve covered themselves from each other, and they covered themselves from God. As soon as sin came into the picture, instantaneously, they no longer had a right relationship with themselves or with each other because of their shame. Then God came walking in the garden, and they were frightened, so they covered themselves. They thought hiding in the bushes was going to work. I have news for you. You can't hide from God. But they didn't know that yet. "So they hid from the LORD God among the trees. Then the LORD God called to the man, 'Where are you?' He replied, 'I heard you walking in the garden, so I hid. I was afraid because I was naked'" (vv. 8–10).

I want you to take note of God's response: "Who told you that you were naked?" (v. 11). It's not God who tells us there's something wrong in our lives; it's sin. Sin not only shames us; it tells us there's no cure for our problem.

God asked, "Have you eaten from the tree whose fruit I commanded you not to eat?" (v. 11). After some blaming and excuses, Adam and Eve finally admitted, *"Yes, we did, Lord."*

Because of this one decision, our whole lives were transformed in a negative way—forever. We are separated from God, and we are separated from each other. Even the greatest love relationships struggle because of sin. Think about how many marriages in America today end in divorce. Your spouse is the person you claim to love more than anyone else. And even when you have a child, you love that child so much, you think, *I could never imagine being frustrated with this sweet, amazing child.* Give them time. They will grow. Every child is beautiful, and it's wonderful when they are born, but look out. That separation will show itself.

Why? Sin affects us. It affects every relationship regardless of what that relationship is. Sin is right there.

How to Make Things Right

So what happens now that sin has entered the picture? Is there anything you and I can do to repair our broken relationships?

To have a right relationship with God and others, you and I have to uncover things about ourselves by asking the following three questions.

How Do I Perceive Life?

The first thing you need to uncover about yourself is, "How do I perceive life?" I don't know if you've noticed, but we don't all see life the same way. If you don't believe me, look at Fox News, and then look at CNN. If you look at both of those news channels, you would think they're covering news in two completely different countries. The number one news story is very rarely the same.

We see things differently not only politically, but because of our ethnic background, our socioeconomic status, our gender, and many other factors. We can each perceive the same event differently. For example, my wife and I can be in the same place, at the same time, and we can see two completely different things and interpret them in completely different ways.

Here's one of the secrets to life: We don't all see the same thing. What we see is affected by who we are.

Jesus said, "Your eye is like a lamp that provides light for your body" (Matthew 6:22). When your eyes are healthy, your whole body is full of light. When your eyes are good, you're going to see everything in a way that is good. But when they are bad, your body is full of darkness. Sin not only affects who we are, but it affects what we see.

We don't always see things accurately. Even if we see a part of the truth, we don't see the whole truth. That's why we need community. We need to be around other people to learn that people are different and see things differently. Different things encourage them, and different things frustrate them; and we have to discover that for ourselves.

You might not even be aware of what you see—of how you experience life or look at life.

In this book, we are going to dig into how each of us perceives life. This is so important because, again, if your spiritual eyes are bad, your view of God is going to be inaccurate. If your eyes are bad, your view of others is going to be distorted. Look at our world today; look at how quickly we judge everyone. We think we know what someone else is thinking or feeling or wants to do. We think we see accurately when we don't. It's one of the main reasons I believe Jesus was constantly restoring sight to the blind. In John 9:41, he told a group of Pharisees, "If you were blind, you wouldn't be guilty. . . . But you remain guilty because you claim you can see." He was saying that although their eyes had nothing wrong with them, they were seeing from their perspective something entirely different than reality.

Think about this: In John 9, Jesus performed a miracle and restored sight to a man who had been born blind. The blind man could now see. When that happened, some people saw a work of

God. Do you know what others saw? The work of the Devil. The same miracle, the same thing happened—same person and two completely different perceptions of what took place.

How Do I Process What I've Perceived?

The second thing you need to uncover about yourself is, "How do I process what I've perceived?" It's not just that we see things differently, but we process things differently. Processing is so important. It's asking, "What does this mean? How do I feel about this? What's going on? What does this mean about me, my family, and my safety? What does this mean about where I am and what I'm doing?"

It's not the events that destroy your life; it's the meaning that we attach to those events. Our perception of an event may or may not be accurate, but when we attach a meaning to it, it can be debilitating. It can destroy us. Some people see an event like a national disaster and ask, "How could a good God allow such evil in the world?" Then they process it and say, "There is no good God." They have perceived something, they've processed it, but they've come to an inaccurate conclusion based on their point of view.

That is why Scripture is so important. We need the Bible because the Bible challenges what we perceive. It challenges the way we process. As Christians, our job is to change the way we think, act, and feel. We have to be different because we don't naturally have the eyes of Jesus, and we don't have the feelings of Jesus. And because of that, often we don't act like Jesus. We act like ourselves. We act like our personality, according to our needs and our wants. What is sad is that sometimes we act in a way we don't even want to because we don't understand ourselves. In the following chapters, you are going to learn some things about yourself that you never knew, simply because you'll begin the process of looking and saying, "God, I want you to show me what I've been missing."

How Do I Present Myself?

Finally, the third thing you need to uncover is, "How do I present myself?" Because you perceive the world in a certain way, and then you process it in a certain way, you present yourself to other people in a certain way.

For example, I didn't realize for a long time that I was a close talker. I tend to get into people's personal space when I talk to them. People have said that I stare into their souls. Well, part of it is because I have ADD. If I'm not staring at your face, I'm looking at everything else, and people feel like I'm not paying attention. I also realize we live in a culture where people don't make eye contact, so when I stare, people freak out. I've had to learn to present myself as a person who wants people to know I care about them, so I stare at their faces, and it makes them very uncomfortable. I was unaware of how I presented myself for years until I met a psychologist who said, "You're a close talker, and it makes me feel uncomfortable. I need you to take a step back." Now I've become more aware of how I present myself, and I notice that people get uncomfortable if I'm too close, and I've learned to step back. It was something I had been doing my entire life, but I never knew until someone helped me see how I was presenting myself.

We all do this to some extent. We perceive the world in a certain way; we process the information that we're perceiving, and then we present ourselves accordingly. Sometimes we're presenting ourselves as an unfriendly person, even though we want friends. Sometimes we present ourselves as a know-it-all, even though we know we don't know it all. A lot of us are confused about why people are offended by what we say or do. So we have to look at ourselves and ask, "How do people receive me? What do they experience when they interact with me?" This book is going to help you learn how to be aware of how people receive you.

Discovering the Real You

We want to invite God to reveal the real you. Make no mistake; we're going to be in God's Word in every single chapter. We're going to be looking at Scripture, and we're going to ask God to do one thing: "God, would you reveal the real me? Would you show me, me?"

Remember, the Enneagram is just a tool, but God can use this tool to transform your life, to challenge you, and to reveal to you the areas where He needs to remove some dirt. Because of the love of God, because of the grace of Jesus Christ, I pray that you would be able to let God reveal the good.

Some people don't accept the fact that there's any beauty about them at all. I hear people say all the time that they don't have many gifts. They don't have any talents. That's a lie. Every single human being is created in the image of God, and you reflect God in some way. There is something beautiful about you. All of us have gifts and talents, as well as things we shouldn't be doing because they're not for us.

There are some things about ourselves that we'd rather not be honest about. But Jesus can't change me unless I offer up everything to Him.

Some things in my life are really ugly. I remember a fight I had with my wife, Tammy, that I'm not proud of. It was about twenty-three years ago, and I had just started Sandals Church. It was an ugly fight, and she locked herself in the bathroom. I was yelling through the door, and she was crying on the other side of the door. And I actually said these words: "Why is it that the whole world thinks I'm awesome, but you can't stand me?" I'm not proud of it, but it's what I said. And I heard this little whimpering voice from the other side of the door say, "Because no one knows the real you like I do."

It was one of the first times in my life that I heard the word of God, and He spoke through my wife. It was awful, but do you know what? If I was going to be healed in my marriage, I had to get real.

There are some things in every one of our lives that we want to pretend don't exist. But if you really want God to take hold of your life, if you really want God to change your life, you need to be real about the ugly. And we all have it. God is completely uninterested in the way we look on the outside, but He's interested in who we are on the inside.

Look at Psalm 139:23: "Search me, God, and know my heart; test me and know my anxious thoughts" (NIV). A lot of us struggle with anxiety, but we don't have any human understanding about why. I believe God can reveal to you why you struggle with anxiety and present a plan that will help you move forward. Through the Enneagram, I've allowed God to search me. I've asked God to know my heart and to know my anxious thoughts.

Psalm 51:6 says, "Behold, you delight in truth in the inward being, and you teach me wisdom in the secret heart" (ESV). There is truth outside, and there is truth inside. A lot of us are comfortable with principles and philosophies and theories. We are comfortable with things we can discover in the classroom, but we're not comfortable in the heart. But God teaches us "wisdom in the secret heart." There are parts of me that I don't know; they are a secret to me. Some parts of me only God knows, but He wants to reveal those parts to me. There are good things about me that I don't know, and there are some things that I need to correct that I don't know about. I'm going to be honest: even as a pastor, there's still some real ugliness in me that the Lord needs to reveal. But here's the good news—He loves me.

Our sin has caused us to cover ourselves and hide, but we don't have to hide from God, because we have Jesus. We can run to Jesus. He is our protector. He is our defender, and He shields us not only from shame but from the wrath of God. He protects us in all things. It is why Hebrews 4:16 says that we can come to the Lord boldly. We can come to Him in our time of need, because of Jesus.

Psalm 119:29 says, "Keep me from lying to myself; give me the privilege of knowing your instructions." This verse is hard for me, and you'll know more about that once we study Enneagram type Three—because that's what I am. Lying to myself is a struggle I have every day. Some of us struggle with this, and we're not willing to deal with the real truth. A lot of us don't just lie to others, but we lie to ourselves. We've convinced ourselves that this is as good as it gets—nothing can ever change, and nothing we do matters. We've created all these lies that imprison us.

Jesus said in John 8:32, "You will know the truth, and the truth will set you free" (ESV). My prayer in this book is that you will be set free to be who God called you to be. Some of you are struggling in your marriages like Tammy and I did. You're struggling and fighting over the same issue over and over again. The Enneagram helped release us from that prison of having the same fight over and over again. Not only will you discover who you are, but you'll discover who your spouse is and who your friends are. And when you understand the way you're wired, you'll be able to communicate with them and create a language that makes it easier to be real. It is not easy to be real, but it's what God has called us to do, and this book will make it easier for you.

In this book you will be reminded why God loves you. We have all wondered from time to time if we are worthy of His love, asking ourselves, *Why does God love me? Why did God send His Son to die on the cross for me? Why do I matter so much to God?* You see, the Bible isn't just all about God; it's all about God's love for you, for me, for us. For a lot of us, even those of us who call ourselves Christians, it's really hard for us to say, "Yeah, God loves me. I matter. This is who I am." The reality is you have value, and you are worthy of love. That's why Jesus died for you on the cross. God loves you, God sent His Son to die for you on the cross, God cares about you, and God wants to transform and change you, He wants to enhance the beauty that's in you, and He wants to begin to heal the brokenness that's in all of us.

At this point, you may be tempted to check out and think the Enneagram just sounds like self-help. But what is wrong if something actually helps? I believe God is for anything that helps us to become more real with Him, with each other, and with ourselves. The Bible says, "Whatever is true, whatever is noble, whatever is right, whatever is pure, whatever is lovely, whatever is admirable—if anything is excellent or praiseworthy—think about such things" (Philippians 4:8 NIV). That's what we will be doing in this book. We're focusing on you, getting you to see the real you—the good, the bad, and the ugly.

I truly believe God is going to do an amazing thing through this book. I believe God is going to bring a revival of love for ourselves. I believe when we start loving ourselves, we are going to be contagious in a good way—to everyone we know and everyone with whom we interact. We live in a world where people hate themselves. They hate what they look like, who they are, and what they do. But God wants to set you free from that prison. He wants to set you up for a life of love in which you not only believe that God loves you, but you actually live like it.

> *Heavenly Father, I know many people who are saying, "I'm not worthy of love." Would You, through Your Holy Spirit, speak truth to them? God, I pray that every single one of us would ask You, "What are You inviting me to learn about myself in this book? What do You need to change in me? God, how do You need to redirect me? What are the things in my life You need to affirm? God, what are the good and kind words that need to be spoken over me?" Lord, I pray that You would invite us all in a very real way to become as real as we've ever been. We pray this in Jesus' name, amen.*

THE REFORMER

Goodness vs. Anger

I don't know if you've noticed, but we're different. Have you noticed that? We come from different ethnicities. We come from different socioeconomic backgrounds. We have different genders. We come from different worlds. Even if you were raised in the same home, have you ever looked at your brother or sister and thought, *Where were you raised?* I'll listen as my brother talks about our childhood, and I'll be like, "I don't know where that was."

And of course, we see things differently. Not everybody sees the world the same way you do. If you're married, there are two sets of eyes looking at the same thing, but you each see it differently. We perceive the world differently, and then we process what we perceive very differently. *Here's what I thought I saw, and here's how that makes me feel.* And then, you'll remember, we present ourselves to other people in a certain way.

This book is about you. God loves you, God sent His Son to

die for you on the cross, God cares about you, and God wants to transform and change you. He wants to enhance the beauty that's in you, and He wants to heal the brokenness that's in all of us. The Enneagram is about you, too, so let's dig in.

We're going to start our discussion of the Enneagram with the personality style I call the Reformer. This is also called "the good person." The type One, the Reformer, is the person who sees how things could be. They're perfectionists.

Now, this is not me. I have zero perfectionist in me. But my wife has a lot of One in her. This is why she always wants to make sure she looks good. I just assume I am good. I look in the mirror and think, *This is what you get. Let's just go.* I don't change outfits. I just want to get out the door.

Ones want to be good. They are led by a deep internal compass. It's a compass they are not always aware of, but it guides them. Ones are led by instinct. As Ones, they just know how the world should be. As Ones, they want the world to be a better place. So they see flaws. They see how things could be different, and they want to change things to be better.

Ones in the Bible: The Prodigal Son's Older Brother

To learn more about Ones, we're going to look at an amazing story from Jesus. Even if you know this story, you may not have recognized this unique personality in one of its characters.

The story begins in Luke 15:11: "Jesus told them this story: 'A man had two sons.'" How sad is it that for two thousand years we've called this story "the parable of the prodigal son"? It's not a story about one son; it's a story about two sons. We focus all the attention on the son who screwed up and then got his life right and had a right relationship with his father in the end. We completely forget about the other son. But Jesus said this is a story about *two* kids. (Parents, your kids are going to be different, so you have to treat them differently, you have to love them differently, and you have to approach them differently.)

Here's the story Jesus told: "A man had two sons. The younger son told his father, 'I want my share of your estate now before you die.' So his father agreed to divide his wealth between his sons" (vv. 11–12). The son was saying, "Dad, you're lasting longer than I thought you would. I want my inheritance now, so give me my money." What's amazing is that the father agreed, so he divided his wealth between his two sons. Now, in the ancient world, the oldest son would get two-thirds of the estate, and the younger son would get one-third. If there were sisters involved, then the sister would get a dowry, some money set aside to make her more appealing for marriage. So the younger son's inheritance was chopped up based on the order he was born. Right off the top, he lost two-thirds of the money to his older brother. Then he got his one-third, minus any sisters they had. If you are a type One, this has wrecked you because of the injustice of it all, but try and keep reading.

So the younger son took his money and went off and partied. After his wild living, he had lost all his money. He went crazy. That is often what happens when young people gain wealth. They didn't earn it, and they don't know how to handle it, so their lives begin to fall apart. When the son finally came to his senses, he said to himself, "At home even the hired servants have food enough to spare, and here I am dying of hunger!" (v. 17). He realized, *I've made a mistake. This is not working out well.* Have you ever been there?

When people ask me, "Why do you follow God?" I say, "Well, I tried to follow myself. I was really good at it. I was good at following myself and the desires of my heart. But it always led to disaster."

The younger son realized that at home, even the hired servants had food enough to spare. He said, "I will go home to my father and say, 'Father, I have sinned against both heaven and you, and I am no longer worthy of being called your son. Please take me on as a hired servant'" (vv. 18–19). The son planned out his apology before he went home.

So, the younger son returned home to his father, and while he was still a long way off, his father saw him coming. Filled with love and compassion, the father ran to his son, he embraced him, and he kissed him. The son said, "Father, I've sinned against both heaven and you, and I am no longer worthy of being called your son" (v. 21). The father stopped him. He didn't make him run through the whole speech. Instead, his father said to his servants, "Quick! Bring the finest robe in the house and put it on him. Get a ring for his finger and sandals for his feet" (v. 22).

The father said, *"Bring the finest robe in the house."* This was not the robe the younger son left behind. This was the robe reserved for visiting royalty and wealthy guests. He said, *"Get a ring for his finger."* The ring symbolizes the permanence of family. He was not a slave; he was a son. He said, *"Get sandals for his feet."* In the ancient world, one of the ways you could tell a slave from a son is with shoes. The father continued, "We must celebrate with a feast, for this son of mine was dead and has now returned to life. He was lost, but now he is found" (vv. 23–24).

Not long ago, Tammy and I were invited to the White House. We got to be a part of a visit where we were briefed by the president's staff. They talked about some of the issues religious people are facing around the world. As we were sitting in the White House at this briefing, a cabinet member shared, "My daughter is missing." She is in one of the most powerful positions in the world, but she can't find her child. So we prayed for her right there.

What is interesting is that no matter how powerful you are, no matter what your position is, when your kid is missing, life isn't right. That's how the dad felt in this story. It didn't matter how successful he was, and it didn't matter how blessed he had become, he was missing a kid. He thought his son was dead, but he turned up alive. He thought the kid was gone forever, but now he was home. It was time to party because the son who was lost had been found! And so the party began.

Meanwhile, how many sons were there? Two. There were two sons. One son rebelled, but the other one was the kid everybody wants. He was the good kid. He always did the right thing. He was the kid who does well in school. He was the kid whose parents have the bumper sticker: "My son is an outstanding student at so-and-so school."

The older son was doing exactly what he was supposed to be doing. That is what Ones do. They get stuff done. And thank God for them! If you are ever tempted to be critical of these good people, remember that without them, there's no church. Do you know why? Ones serve. They tithe. They come. They are faithful. Some people say, "I don't know if we're going to go to church this weekend. I have to feel it." But not Ones. They say, "It is the Lord's day. We are going to church." Thank God for the Ones.

Can you imagine what the world would be like if we didn't have good people? What if everybody drove on the highway like you did? This week, I watched someone turn around accidentally and drive the wrong direction on the freeway. I don't even know how that was possible! Think about it: what are you usually doing in your car? I can tell you what the Ones are doing. The Ones, the Reformers, they are driving—they're not on their phones, they're not texting; they're praying for your soul. They are good, they work hard, and they get stuff done.

So, the older brother was in the field working. When he returned home, he heard the music and saw the dancing in the house. He asked one of his servants, *"What's going on?"* " 'Your brother is back,' he was told, 'and your father has killed the fattened calf. We are celebrating because of his safe return'" (v. 27). It was a full-on party.

But the older brother wouldn't go in. Why? It wasn't fair. Ones are monitoring. They're keeping score. They're like the world's referees, crying, "Foul!"

My wife has a lot of One in her personality. We will be in line at the airport, when someone cuts in line. She'll cry, "Foul!" I'll tell her, "It's going to be okay; we're going to make it." She'll protest, "But he is cutting! It's not fair."

If you have a child who is a One, you've experienced this. When you pour cereal for your kids, the first thing the Ones do is evaluate. They make sure all the portions are equal before anyone eats. Right? They say, "The cereal bowls should be fair!"

The older brother was angry, and he wouldn't go into the party. His father came out and begged him, *"Come on, son."* The good son said, "All these years I've slaved for you and never once refused to do a single thing you told me to" (v. 29). If you're a One, you could say something like this too: "I do everything right." And Ones, thank God for you. We need you. We love you.

The good brother said to the father, "In all that time you never gave me even one young goat for a feast with my friends" (v. 29). He was probably thinking, *You killed a cow for my idiot kid brother, but*

I don't even get a goat for a feast with my friends. "Yet when this son of yours comes back after squandering your money on prostitutes, you celebrate by killing the fattened calf" (v. 30). Notice that he calls him "this son of yours," not "my brother." And how did he know his brother was squandering money on prostitutes? Regardless, now they were celebrating by killing a fattened calf.

His father said to him, "Look, dear son, you have always stayed by me" (v. 31). Ones, God sees what you do. And you will be rewarded. One day God will measure out in proportion to how you served, but today is not that day for the good son. Today is about his brother. He was dead, and now he's alive, and that's something to celebrate.

The father continued, "Everything I have is yours" (v. 31). Now, this is significant. That's actually true. Remember, the story began with the father dividing his assets. So the father was actually taking the fatted calf *from the oldest son.* It's the good son's cow, and the father was giving it to the prodigal son. What do you think that felt like to the good son? Ones will say it's stealing. *"Dad, you divided the estate between us, and Junior blew all his money. I invested my portion, and that's why the calf is fat."*

Jesus concluded his story with this statement from the father to the good son: "We had to celebrate this happy day. For your brother was dead and has come back to life! He was lost, but now he is found!" (v. 32).

The Character of Ones: They Reflect God's Goodness

If you are a One, the first thing I want to challenge you to do is to praise God that He made you a One. From the moment you were born, God gave you a desire to do what is right, and that's beautiful. We need the person who sees the world the way it should be. They make the world a better place because they are constantly improving.

Ones reflect God's goodness. Do we need more goodness in the world? Yes! We need to praise God for these good kids who reflect the goodness of God. They care about what's right. They care about what's true. This is how you reflect your Maker.

First Peter 2:9 says, "You are a chosen people. You are royal priests, a holy nation, God's very own possession. As a result, you can show others the goodness of God, for he called you out of the darkness into his wonderful light." As a One, you can show others the goodness of God. Ones, this is what you do—you show people there is good in the world. You do what is right, even when you don't feel like it. There is no kingdom of God on earth without you. You serve. You give. You tithe. You show up. You build. And you do the right thing when everybody else is doing the stupid thing. Thank God for you. You are God's possession, and as a result, you can show others the goodness of God.

But notice 1 Peter 2:9 also says that God has "called you out of the darkness." If you're the good person, what's your darkness that God's calling you out of? None of us is perfect, even if we strive for perfection. So if you're a good person, let me ask you this question: What's your sin? What I find to be so tragic is that Ones, especially if they grew up in the church, think they don't have a good testimony. They think their testimony is lame. They don't have a dramatic story about being saved from a Las Vegas, heroin, and prostitute lifestyle. And it's tragic, right?

Not at all! It's tragic that in the church we've focused on the prodigal son story, and we fail to understand that both sons needed the gospel for different reasons. Both sons were lost. One son was an idiot, but the other was judgmental.

Here's the thing: I don't believe this story was ever about the prodigal son. Do you know why I don't believe that? Because his whole life is fixed. We know everything that happened to him. But we don't know how it ends with the good son. What happened to him? Remember, this is a parable, a made-up story. Jesus wasn't talking about this boy; he was talking about you. He's asking you, *Can you trust Me? Can you trust that I'll be good to you like I am to these prodigals who come to Me? Can you trust Me that I'm going to reward you for your faithfulness?*

Here's how Satan tempts Ones: "Is God really good?" Is the father in the story really good? Is what he's doing really wise? If you're a One, not only does the son think his brother is an idiot; he thinks his father might be one too. And that's a sin. The Bible says God has called you out of the darkness and into his wonderful light.

The Core Motivation of Ones: Goodness

What's your core motivation if you are a One? To do what is good and right. You ask, "What's the right thing to do?" before you ask, "What do I want to do?"

Most of us say, "Well, I'm going to do whatever feels good." Not Ones. Ones say, "We'll get to feelings later. First, we're going to do what's right. We're going to make sure everybody's in their appropriate box. We're going to make sure everything's in line, and everything has to be good and right."

Ones Need to Be Perfect

What is the core need of the One? To be perfect. Good luck with that.

Ones Focus on Flaws

What does the One focus on? Flaws. Ones, all you see are your flaws.

As I said, my wife has a lot of One in her. She got her hair cut this week. She said, "Do you like my hair?" I told her, "I like you. We're good. Hair, no hair. Short, blonde, or whatever is great." Because what my wife tends to see is how beautiful she's not. What she needs to be reminded of is how beautiful she is. That's what we have to do for Ones. They don't give themselves or anyone else any grace. They focus on their flaws, and guess what that does? It creates their core sin: anger.

The Core Sin of Ones: Anger

What was the older brother's response to the party? He was angry, and he refused to go in.

"Your brother's alive. How does that make you feel?"
"That ticks me off. If life was fair, he'd be dead."

The core sin of Ones is anger.

Ones Avoid Criticism

What does the One have to avoid at all costs? Criticism. Here's the thing: if you're a One, do you know who you're the most critical of? Yourself. You have the least amount of grace for yourself. Ones can be very critical of their children, their spouses, and their friends. They can be very critical of their employers or their employees.

This is what Ones do. They "should" all over themselves and others: *You should. I should. They should.* Ones, you need to stop should-ing on everybody.

Ones Fear Being Flawed

And here's the other thing: your core fear, if you're a One, is being flawed—and guess what you are? Flawed. So your nightmare is like every day over and over and over again. You're not perfect. You will never be perfect, and the harder you try, the worse you're going to get.

How Ones Can Be Real with
Self, Others, and God

How can you be real with yourself, others, and God if you're a One?

Real with Self

Ones, to be real with yourself, you need to remember this: nobody is perfect. The One's favorite Bible verse might be Matthew 5:48: "You are to be perfect, even as your Father in heaven is perfect." Do you know why we have that in our Bibles? Because of a Catholic priest named Jerome. Jerome's problem was that he fell in love with a nun. Some smoking-hot sister was in Rome, and it was affecting his holy life. So he confessed it to his bishop, and his bishop said, "As penance [a Catholic term for repenting], you will go to Bethlehem and learn Hebrew." So Jerome went to Bethlehem, to the place where they believed Jesus was born, he buried himself in a cave, and he learned Hebrew. He translated the Hebrew Scriptures into Latin, and when he came to this Greek word *telos*, he translated it as "perfect": "Be perfect as your Father in heaven is perfect." Now, every Bible translation is built upon and influenced by a previous translation. So for almost seventeen hundred years, we translated the word *telos* that way, going all the way back to Jerome, who said, "Be perfect as your Father in heaven is perfect." The problem is, *telos* doesn't mean "perfect." It means "whole, complete." Ones, it doesn't mean you need to make the perfect pie. It means to make sure you have all the slices. It means to be complete as God is complete. What you're missing is God's grace for you and others.

So, Ones, don't make Matthew 5:48 your favorite verse. Instead, I suggest Ephesians 4:26: "'Don't sin by letting anger control you.' Don't let the sun go down while you are still angry." Some of you Ones are thinking, *Well, then, I would never sleep. That's how I go to sleep at night. I count all the sins of my spouse. I count the sins of others. I don't count sheep; I count sins. One, two, three, four . . .*

But trust me. You can do it.

Real with Others

Ones, *to be real with others, you need to stop focusing on other people's sins.* You're not perfect, and neither is anybody else. Why do you think the younger brother in Jesus' story is an idiot? Because we're all idiots compared to you, Ones. Jesus is a genius; He knows precisely what ticks you off. Ones, you are ticked off by idiots who are screwing up their lives by making wrong choices. You're saying, *God, I know You have a list in heaven, but we will compare notes when I get there, and we will make sure that every sin is accounted for.*

Here's the problem: when you focus on the sins of others, it makes you angry. When you allow anger in your life, it gives the

Devil an opportunity in your life. It "gives a foothold to the devil" (Ephesians 4:27). All-encompassing anger is not even close to perfection; it's evil. Don't sin by letting anger control you. You can be angry, but don't let it get hold of you; don't let it destroy you.

Ones' pursuit of perfection can destroy their marriages. You can want a perfect marriage and destroy the one you have. You can want perfect children and ruin them. You have to learn to relax. Sometimes just go into the pantry and move the beans over to the rice. Go crazy and put a chocolate bar over by the crackers.

So, Ones, what will you do when you hear, "There is a party at your house!" Just embrace it. Embrace life. Because your desire for perfection will ruin you. It will destroy you. It will wreck you. Your kids will never be perfect. Your company, your clothes, and your church will never be perfect. We're going to screw it up. We're going to mess it up. There's a bloody cross with a dead Jesus on it that says nobody's perfect. Nobody's perfect; that's why we're Christians.

So remember: "'Don't sin by letting anger control you.' Don't let the sun go down while you are still angry, for anger gives a foothold to the devil" (Ephesians 4:26–27). Ones, this is your confession every night before you go to bed: "God, help me to forgive this imperfect world that's not fair." This world is not fair, but God is good.

Ones, here's the question for you as the good son: Do you trust your Father? Who knows best, you or Dad? That's what Jesus' story is asking. Well, if you're a One, you are convinced you know what's best, and God would do well to listen to your wisdom. But let me ask you this, Ones: who gave you your wisdom? God did. Trust Him.

If you are a One, here's a verse for how you relate to others: "Make allowance for each other's faults" (Colossians 3:13). You may

have a brother who makes stupid mistakes. You might marry someone who does idiotic things. My wife has prayed this verse many
times. She did not marry a One—she married the prodigal son.
She strapped herself to an idiot forever. "Make allowance for each
other's faults." It's why I'm a professional apologizer. Do you know
what the hardest thing is for a One to do? Say "I'm sorry." Because
that means you have to admit you were wrong. What happened?
You're human. One time I said something dumb to my wife (and I
don't recommend this). I said, "Just say it."

She said, "What?"

"Just say you're wrong. I'll help you. I say it all the time: 'I'm
wrong. I screwed up. I'm sorry.'" That feels so good. That's empow-
ering. But not for a One.

Colossians 3:13 says, "Make allowance for each other's faults,
and forgive anyone who offends you. Remember, the Lord forgave
you, so you must forgive others." Ones get offended. They say,
"That is offensive." Ones, you're the offensive police. Why do you
need to learn to forgive people? Because the Lord Jesus forgave
you. For what? Your sin. And what's your sin? For a lot of Ones,
it's self-righteousness. Self-righteousness believes that you are right
within yourself. Righteousness comes from God, and only God is
truly right. Only God is truly good. So it's okay for you to make a
mistake. It's okay for you to screw it up. It's okay for you to mess
up. We have a wonderful Savior and a wonderful God who can
forgive us, and I hope there are Christians in your life who can
extend grace to you too.

A One's greatest fear is that someone's going to treat them
the way they treat themselves. You're afraid you will be criticized,
blamed, judged, and not measure up. It's okay, Ones. We know
you're better than we are, but you're not perfect. We praise God

for how awesome you are. But you're still a sinner, and you're still going to blow it. You can do your very best and still have a screwed-up marriage. You can do your very best and still struggle at work, struggle in friendships, and struggle at family relationships. Sometimes your best isn't good enough. Do you know what you need? Grace. You can have good intentions and still sin.

What Ones will do instead of saying, "I'm sorry," is say, "Well, what I meant to do is . . ." They'll say, "I didn't mean to slay your heart. What I meant to do was to say, 'Wouldn't you look better in a different outfit?'" When your kid has seven A's and all you talk about is the B minus, that's the One in you. Don't try to make your kids be something you can't be yourself—they're not perfect.

Make allowance for each other's faults. Everyone who drives is an idiot, right? You can always identify Ones on the freeway—they're looking around and judging. If you want to see something funny, put a One in the passenger seat. If I didn't have to keep all my attention on the road not to kill my family, I would just watch my wife while I drive.

Real with God

How can Ones be real with God? If you grew up in the church, you've heard people say, "God is good, all the time." Only God is good all the time. Ones, you're good most of the time. But God is good *all* the time. Psalm 86:15 says, "You, O Lord, are a God of compassion and mercy, slow to get angry and filled with unfailing love and faithfulness."

Ones, isn't it good to know that God is faithful to us when we screw up? Aren't you glad that God can enter into a beautiful, wonderful relationship with us that is perfect because of Christ, even when we are imperfect? Remember, if you are a One, your core sin is anger. You have to pursue grace. How do you do that? Well, think about this: how does God deal with His anger for sinners? He poured His grace over us on the cross. So how do you deal with your anger? You ask God to give you grace for yourself and for others.

Ones, in your darkest moments, you're likely going to accuse God of not being good. You may doubt God in your lowest moments because life does not always make sense. But here's the difference: Ones see rules. Jesus sees souls. Ones are trying for perfection. Jesus is trying to save souls. In Jesus' parable, the father said, "We had to celebrate this happy day. For your brother was dead and has come back to life!" (Luke 15:32). God is inviting us to celebrate—and Ones, He's inviting you to the party. Don't let your anger keep you from the party. God is inviting you. He's begging you. Please come to the party. The One in the story missed the party, but you don't have to!

How Do You Love a One?

Ones are good people, but they can be really challenging to love well. The reason is, they are consumed with what's wrong and have a hard time enjoying what's right. Try these ideas.

1. Compliment them!

Ones are consumed with criticism. I know it may feel like they are always criticizing you, but that's just the tip of the iceberg of how much they criticize themselves.

So I suggest you learn to aggressively compliment. If they are a struggling One, they will hate it. But their soul is desperate for it. A good friend of mine is married to a One. Of course, he thinks she is beautiful, which she is. Sometimes he likes to stare at her. That's weird, unless it's your wife. She hates it, because when she looks into the mirror, all she sees are her flaws. We all have them, but Ones become overwhelmed by them. Don't give ground. Ones will push back, but you must push forward. A child who is a One will insist they are dumb, ugly, useless. You must be the loving voice who states that's not true. Ones see a mistake as total and absolute failure; you must firmly and lovingly help them see the good in themselves. Remember, they are usually better than the rest of us, so it shouldn't be that hard.

2. Help them finish tasks.

Ones love lists. They have lists for themselves, lists for you, and maybe even a list for God (called prayer requests). Lists are important. For Ones, make sure they know they are a priority for you. Ones wake up every day seeing an imperfect world that needs tidying up! Their lists can be overwhelming. Listen, husband of a One: if you want to get on your wife's list of things that need *to get done* . . . then make sure her list is done.

You can start helping a One by helping them narrow down their list; after all, they have an entire lifetime to fix us and everything else! Lovingly help them discover the joy of making lists that can actually get done. When the list is done, Ones can actually relax, and then there will be time for you to enjoy this wonderful person.

3. Be a person of integrity.

Ones feel loved when you do what's right. Ones have a deep sense of what's right and what's wrong. They have a hard time feeling loved by people who lack moral character. Make sure you act ethically. And if you are a Christian, act biblically. If you are raising a child who is a One, don't make promises that you can't keep. It's not the making of promises that makes a One feel loved; it's you being able to keep them!

4. Help them have fun.

If a One loves doing something for fun, do it with them and do it often. Running a house is tough work, and my wife runs a tight ship. It takes a lot for her to relax. When I take her skiing, though, she is a different person. She grew up skiing, so it relaxes her . . . and then I make it back on the list (*wink wink*). Here's the thing: don't take a One on a trip where they have tons of things to do! Make sure Ones can actually relax while on vacation.

Ones have a hard time letting their hair down and just chilling. They will never take time off on their own, so you need to help them be intentional about relaxing and enjoying a checklist-free life once in a while. Help them create space and time away from lists, kids, and stress. I remember one unhealthy One in my church told me, "The Devil never takes a day off, and neither do I." But the Devil is not our example to follow—Jesus is! And if you read through the gospels, you'll see that He took time off to get away. If God rested and relaxed, so can Ones!

A Prayer for Ones

If you identify with the One, the Reformer, I challenge you to pray this prayer:

> *God, help me not to seek perfection but to seek You. Help me see others the way You see them, not as perfect but as perfectly loved.*

Ones, that's how God loves you—perfectly. It's not just about getting life right; it's about being complete and whole. He's inviting you to love others in the same way. And here's my prayer for you.

Holy Father, I pray that we would all find grace for ourselves. I know the Ones are spinning with criticism for themselves, so I pray that You would block that criticism and reassure them that even though they're the best among us—the most moral, the most right, and the purest—they're still sinners, and they need grace just like all of us. Help them know that they reflect Your goodness, God, but like all of us, they need Your mercy. I pray that they would find the mercy they need at the cross. In Jesus' name, amen.

THE HELPER

Love vs. Pride

In the previous chapter, we focused on Ones—the Reformers. Ones are people who see the world the way it should be. They make the world a better place because they are constantly improving. That's the beauty of the One. The brokenness of the One is that if they're not careful, they can become critical and negative. They tell everybody what's wrong with everything.

The Two is called the Helper. We love these people. Why? They help us and they serve us. They were Girl Scouts or Boy Scouts. Today, they volunteer at their kids' schools. At church, Twos are the first to jump up to serve. If you're moving, the Two shows up to help you, to come alongside and serve you. This is who they are.

There would be no church without the Twos. The Twos serve so you can attend the worship service. They work in the parking lot so when you pull in, they can help you find a space so that you can maybe get saved and go to heaven. So thank God for them. And thank them for what they do.

Twos in the Bible: Martha

In this chapter, we're going to look at a Two in the Bible. Her name is Martha.

Martha's story begins in Luke 10:38: "As Jesus and the disciples continued on their way to Jerusalem, they came to a certain village, where a woman named Martha welcomed him into her home." Thank God for Martha; she had room for Jesus. Some people have no room for Jesus in their homes or in their hearts. But Martha had room for Jesus in her home, so she welcomed Him over.

"Her sister, Mary, sat at the Lord's feet, listening to what he taught" (v. 39).

Let me just say this: if you have kids and you're raising boys, praise God. You know when boys don't like each other, right? Somebody's bleeding, something is broken, someone may be going to jail—that's what happens when you raise boys. When you raise girls, it's like North Korea. You never know when the nuke is coming—they're ready to kill us all.

So in Luke 10, we see two sisters. Martha is the one who welcomes Jesus to her home. And her sister Mary is the cute, social butterfly. (No, it doesn't say that in the text. I'm reading that in there.)

Do you know where women went to school two thousand years ago? The University of Nowhere. Two thousand years ago, a woman didn't have legal rights. Her testimony was not valid in a court of law. She was seen as a second-class citizen, and her entire identity was wrapped up in her father, her husband, or her brother. Women were not allowed to learn.

But Jesus taught women. He accepted them and allowed them to sit right next to the boys, and He began to teach them. Mary was taking advantage of this opportunity. She sat at the Lord's feet, listening to what He taught.

The next verse says, "But Martha was distracted by the big dinner she was preparing" (v. 40). Notice the big "but" there. Twos are wonderful, beautiful, and amazing. They serve us, and they help us. *But* they are distracted. They can get so wrapped up in the details, and in helping, that they miss opportunities.

Now, let's give Martha some grace. You would be a little nervous if Jesus were eating at your house today, right? If your answer is no, you are a Three, and you're a liar—ha! We're going to talk to you in the next chapter. If you're a Two, you would probably be thinking your meal isn't good enough for Jesus. Can you imagine how stressed out you would be if the Lord Jesus Christ Himself were coming over to your house to enjoy your mom's recipes? You would be uptight.

So Martha was distracted by the big dinner she was preparing. Why? Because Jesus Christ was coming over. *She was feeding God.*

Imagine this: Someone in town asks Martha, "What are you doing today?" She replies, "Oh, you know, just *feeding God*!"

Verse 40 tells us how Martha responded when she saw her sister Mary sitting at Jesus' feet: "She came to Jesus and said, 'Lord, doesn't it seem unfair to you that my sister just sits here while I do all the work? Tell her to come and help me.'" Anybody detect a little unhealthy One here? Remember, in the last chapter, the Ones are the referees. They make sure everybody's doing it correctly. They call the fouls. Ones have to make sure everybody's right; otherwise, the whole world would unravel. Martha said, *"Lord, it's not fair. I'm over here working. I'm over here slaving. But my sister, she's just sitting there while I do all the work."* You can almost hear her exasperation: *It always happens—I do all the work, and Mary gets all the credit.* It's interesting. Later in this chapter, we are going to find out more about this tendency when we get into the core sin of the Two.

Martha was saying, *"Tell her, Jesus. You are in charge of everything, but I have a suggestion, Your Lordship. I know You're busy running the universe and making the sun warm our earth and making trees grow. However, I have noticed something that maybe could use Your attention. Tell Mary to come here and help me."*

Everybody should be serving, and everybody should be helping. That's the way Twos see the world. We should all be working. We should all be volunteers. We should all be soccer moms and soccer dads and baseball dads and baseball moms. We should all help with children's church. We should all be on the parking-lot team. Everyone should get a vest and work. "Tell her to come and help me."

How did Jesus respond? "But the Lord said to her, 'My dear Martha . . .'" (v. 41). Twos, that is how Jesus responds to you. Do you feel that? *My dear Martha.* He continued, "You are worried and upset over all these details!"

I don't know if He said this, but He could have added, "Are you aware that I can fast for forty days? Even Satan knows that I can turn stones to bread—I'm pretty sure I can handle the Crock-Pot."

Jesus said, "My dear Martha, you are worried and upset over all these details! There is only one thing worth being concerned about" (v. 41–42). Twos, how sad would it be if Jesus came to your house and you missed spending time with Him? Twos can get so wrapped up in preparing Christmas dinner that they miss enjoying their family at Christmas. For Twos, it's easy to serve; it's easy to clean the house, it's easy to prepare; it's easy to do dishes. It's hard actually to sit and spend time with people—and God.

Jesus said to Martha, "There is only one thing worth being concerned about. Mary has discovered it, and it will not be taken away from her." This is significant: Jesus said that Mary, a woman, was invited to sit at His feet and learn and hear everything He had to say.

The most important thing that was happening at Martha's house that day was not the food she was preparing, but the food Jesus was serving—His Word. Twos can miss this. If you're a Two, chances are you don't regularly go to the worship service at your church. Instead, you are serving somewhere in the church. Twos will serve at every service, and they will do that every single weekend for the entire year and never once make it into the worship service.

Twos—it's often easy for you to serve a church, but it's hard for you to actually go to church.

The Character of Twos: They Reflect God's Heart for Service

Twos reflect God's heart for service. It's good to serve. We need servers. We need people who work, and we need people who volunteer. If our church didn't have volunteers, we would shut down in one weekend. Do you know why churches have to hire people to do things? We don't have enough Twos who are serving and helping. Twos reflect God's heart for service.

When I became a Christian in college, this is the first Bible verse I memorized, and I never forgot it: "Even the Son of Man came not to be served but to serve others and to give his life as a ransom for many" (Matthew 20:28). Jesus came to serve. You can't worship a Servant and not serve.

But do you know how we treat Twos? We abuse Twos. We take advantage of them. We let them do everything while we do nothing.

When I was a little kid, I used to go to my grandparents' house. My grandpa was Italian. It was a different time and a different place, but when my grandpa's coffee cup would get empty, he would tap his fingers on the table, and my grandma would come in and fill his cup. When I got married, and my coffee cup was empty, I tapped my fingers, and Tammy said, "What's wrong with your fingers? Do you have a twitch?"

My grandma was a Two. She walked around the house asking me, "Did you eat? Are you hungry? Do I need to wipe your nose? What do I need to wipe?" I didn't need a bath; I'd just go to Grandma's house. I'd get clean. That's how she loved. She loved to serve.

Let me make this clear: Some of you will take the Enneagram assessment and find out you don't have any Two in you, or very little. Some of you men might be tempted to say, "Well, I don't have any Two, so I'm not going to help around the house." An attitude like that, gentlemen, will only get you one place: *sleeping on the couch!*

I do not do the dishes at my house because I love doing the dishes. I do the dishes at my home because I love my wife, I love my kids, and I want to stay married. I don't take out the trash because I enjoy the smell of rotting food. I take it out because I love my family, and to be honest, no one else will do it. I don't know about your family, but we don't take out the trash until we cannot get the bag out of the dispenser—that's when we know it's time to change it. My kids will come and see the full trash can and just set trash on top like we're building a trash tower. But I face that trash tower—for love.

The Core Motivation of Twos: Love

The core motivation of Twos is to love and feel loved. They feel loved when they feel useful.

So don't tell a Two to stop serving you; let them serve you. But don't abuse them. If Twos are not careful, they can become codependent because they find their identity in serving, and they lose who they are.

If you're a Two and you're a parent, you've got to prepare yourself for the day your kids move out. You will likely feel like your life is over, and you won't know who you are because your identity is wrapped up in what you do. If you work and you're a Two, there's coming a day when you'll have to retire. They're going to make you go home, and you may not know who you are anymore. You'll lose your identity because who you are has been wrapped up in what you do.

Twos, your identity cannot be wrapped up in what you do. It needs to be wrapped up in who you are. You are a son or a daughter of the King—that's who you are. You're a child of God.

Twos Need to Be Needed

The inner need of Twos—what's driving them, what's fueling them—is this: they need to be needed.

My daughter has a lot of Two in her. She said to me, "Dad, I just don't feel like you need me."

I said, "I don't."

Does anybody feel like, *Man, I need some more teenagers around—we're running a little short?* I said to her, "I don't need you, baby girl, but I love you."

I have news for you: did you know that God doesn't need you? God's not up in heaven, saying, "Oh, what am I going to do? I know, I'll create people to help Me make the world go 'round." God doesn't need you, but He loves you.

True love is not codependent. I told my daughter, "I love you. I care for you. I want to be in a relationship with you." But Twos need to be needed. They need to know: What's my role? What's my purpose? *If I'm not a wife, who am I? If I'm not a husband, who am I? If I don't have kids, who am I? If I don't have grandkids, what does it say about me? If I can't walk around constantly helping and serving people, I don't know who I am.*

Twos, it's okay to love serving, but you need to know you're more than that. God didn't just create you for service. He created you, Marthas, for relationship. And Mary chose the right thing. So unplug the Crock-Pot and sit at the table and learn. You're invited.

Here's how you know the Twos in your small group. As soon as the sharing gets deep, they go do the dishes. They go clean. Twos love to serve. For a Two, the safest part of the party is preparing and cleaning. Everything in between is terrifying because there's nothing to do, and it's awkward if you just go and start helping people. That's why, as a Two, you struggle when your kids don't need you as much. I'm actually looking forward to that point in my life. But for Twos, it's scary.

"You don't need me?"

"No, Mom, I'm forty. I'm good."

Twos Focus on the Needs of Others

What's their focus? Here's how Twos can get lost. They're focused on the needs of others. Now, thank God for the Twos. Because without the Twos, we would completely ignore everybody. Twos see needs.

They see the needs of others; they care, and they run in to help. When you're moving, do you know who shows up? The Twos. None of your other friends show up. But Twos say, "Hey, I'm here. What do you need? How can I help? What's going on?" When you have cancer, Twos are there. "How can I help you? How can I serve you?" Because when it gets uncomfortable for the rest of us, the Twos feel very safe. Twos are beautiful, wonderful, amazing people. When my wife's dad was dying of cancer, all the Twos in our lives were around, because cancer, in the end, is really ugly. Twos don't care because they love you. They reflect the heart of God. God still loves you even when you smell like death, and so does a Two.

The Core Sin of Twos: Pride

What is the core sin of the Two? If you're a Two, your sin is the hardest sin of any of the personality types to identify. If you're a One, we know when you're angry; even if you don't know, we know. But Twos struggle with pride.

The hardest sin to detect is the sin of pride. Pride is what made the Devil who he is. You're not called to be like the Devil; you're called to be like Christ. Pride is the one sin that the Bible says God always opposes. If you are wrestling with pride, you are wrestling with God, and you will lose. You say, "Well, I just want to help people." So did Martha, but her pride got the best of her.

Martha thought she knew better than Jesus did. She thought she knew what Mary needed to be doing. Think about that, Twos. Remember, she said, "Jesus, tell her to come and help me." I am sure she was thinking, *I know there are Ten Commandments, Lord, but we need some more for Mary, and here's the first one—"Get off your butt."* Go ahead, Lord; you're in charge.

Twos Avoid Their Own Needs

Do you know what Martha needed? The Lord. Twos, can you imagine that Jesus Christ Himself comes to your house, and you don't spend any time with Him? How sad is that? That's what Martha did. Martha thought the dishes and the plates and the food were more important than Jesus. Twos avoid their own needs.

Twos Fear Being Unworthy

I don't know what happened to you when you were a kid, but we're all a little broken. None of our parents is perfect. I'm not a perfect parent. I tell my kids, "Your first ten counseling sessions are on me." My girls have some unhealthy sense of fear, and I contributed to that. When my daughters were little, I made them watch *The Lord of the Rings.* I'm not proud of it. My girls sometimes share stories of what I made them watch, and I'm like, "You know, girls, there are inside family stories, and there are outside family stories." At the time, I thought it was funny to show them that movie. I don't know what was wrong with me. I'm tweaked. I would go into their bedroom, flip off the lights, and say, "my precious" in my best Sméagol voice.

Because that's what a healthy, loving father does, right? No—wrong! So when they tell that story, I'm like, "Can we not tell that story?" I'm a little bit mortified now.

Twos don't fear Sméagol; they are deeply afraid that if people don't need them, they won't love them. That's their horror film that plays out over and over in their minds. But this fear does not come from being scared; it comes from the underlying emotion of the Two. In the Enneagram there are nine personality types, but only three underlying emotions, and the first two come from the gut and the heart. The Ones are led by their gut. (Remember, Reformers were born with an internal compass. They know right from wrong. They don't even know why; they just know what's right, and they know what's wrong. It's inside them.) But the Twos, Threes, and Fours are led by their hearts. It doesn't mean that they are superior; it just means they are more emotional.

If you married a Two, Three, or Four, you're in for it. My wife has a lot of One and Six gifting. She is not led by her heart. She never cries. I tell her all the time, "You need to leak more." I cry all the time because I'm sensitive. When we watch a sad movie, my kids don't watch the movie; they watch my face: "Dad's crying again!"

The underlying emotion of a Two is shame. If you are a Two, it's likely that something happened inside you in your past where you felt like the only time you're good is when you cover your shame with helping. Let me say this to you. If you're a Two, you can't outwork your shame; only Jesus can.

One of the tragedies of modern psychology in our culture is that for the last forty years in America, we've been teaching kids they should never be ashamed. I don't know if you know this, but sometimes you should feel shame. Sometimes—wait for it, this is deep—you should feel bad.

The modern world says, "You should never feel bad." So we pretend shame isn't real, and look at what's happening to our young people. As a church, we need to accept shame because it's what sin brings. We need to accept our shame so we can take our shame to the cross. If you're a Two, you want to clean the cross of Jesus Christ—there's blood all over it, and you want to make sure it's nice.

But why is that blood there? To wash away your shame. The Twos are ashamed of having needs. They think, *If I were really who I was supposed to be, I wouldn't need anything.* If God didn't think you needed anything, He wouldn't have created others.

The apostle Paul said, "My God will meet all your needs according to the riches of his glory in Christ Jesus" (Philippians 4:19 NIV). God wants you to have needs. It's okay to have needs, and it's okay to need people.

God didn't call you to be Superman; that's why He made Jesus. And by the way, even Jesus said things like, "I thirst." "I need you to pray for Me." "I'm hungry." "I need rest." Even Jesus had needs.

How Twos Can Be Real with
Self, Others, and God

How can Twos learn how to be real?

Real with Self

Here's where I want you to start, Twos—with yourself. It's easy to look at Martha and see where she's whacked. It's hard to look at yourself.

Let me affirm this in Twos: it's good to serve God and family. If you have a Two in your family, you're blessed. They serve you, they take care of you, your world operates wonderfully because of them, and you need to praise God for that. Never tell a Two to stop serving. What we want to change is not their serving. We want to change *why* they serve. We don't want them to serve to try to cover up for something that's missing. We want them to serve just because they enjoy it, because it glorifies God, and because it celebrates God's heart for service.

Twos, when you serve with the right heart, pride will not bring you down; but when you serve with the wrong heart, you start looking around at the rest of us lazy bums, and you start judging all of us. When you come to church, you think, *Look at all these people who aren't serving.* Then you find a One, and you gossip about the rest of us. The One's like, "Yep, they should this, they should that, they should, they should, they should." Or if you're a high One, you sit by yourself and quote Romans 12:11: "Never be lazy, but work hard and serve the Lord enthusiastically."

If you aren't a Two, that doesn't mean you get a pass. You are called to serve. We need you to serve. You're commanded to serve, and you don't have to pray about it. What if your kids and your family treated you the way you treat God? God says to you, "I want you to serve the church." And you respond, "I'm going to pray about that."

What if you said to your kids, "We need you to help out and do chores," and they responded, "I'm gonna get together with the kids at school, and we're gonna pray about whether or not I need to participate in the chores of the family"? How many of you parents would lay hands on your children, right?

It's true that the Bible says, "Never be lazy, but work hard and serve the Lord enthusiastically." It's a privilege to serve God, and I'm amazed that He invites us to participate at all, considering how we screw everything up. So it's good to serve God and our families.

Twos, you may not like this, but in addition to serving God, you also must spend time with God. Spending time with God is not reorganizing your Bible. It's not dusting off your Bible. "Look, my Bible is the cleanest book in the house." Did you read it? "Well, no, but it's clean." If you're a Two, you might go to read the Bible but see all the laundry that needs to be picked up on the way to get your Bible, and before you know it it's four hours later. What happened? No time with God—that's what happened.

Twos keep themselves busy. Do you know why you don't want to stop? Do you know why you don't want to be alone? Because when you're alone, it's you and your shame, you and your feelings—which is a great time to hang out with God. You can say, "God, I feel like crap." And He says, "I know. I've been waiting for you to come to Me about it." God wants you to be honest.

Twos must also spend time with their families. Dads, if you're a Two, that's great; you do all your own yard work. But maybe what your kids need on Saturday is not a mowed lawn. Maybe they need you. Twos will busy themselves with all kinds of things that get in the way of relationship. But Twos, God didn't just design you for service; He designed you for relationship. I know it's scary, but it's scary for all of us. Remember this, Twos—we have to watch how our pride affects the way we see ourselves and others.

Let me be clear about pride. You're not going to deal with it today and then never have to deal with it again. You're going to deal with pride every day for the rest of your life. You're going to defeat pride when you die. When you die, and you stand before Jesus, and He gives you your glorified body, that's when pride will be dead in you. Until that moment, pride is with you every single day, and you need to be aware of that nasty monster because it will devour you.

Obadiah 1:3 states, "You have been deceived by your own pride." We aren't deceived by other people's arrogance. We can see everybody else's pride. We think, *Man, I don't like that person. He is so prideful; he is so arrogant.* But we cannot see our own pride. And it creeps in our lives in weird ways.

Jesus didn't just come to save you from the wrong things you do in your life. He came to save you from the right things you do in your life for the wrong reasons. That's what the Bible means when it says even on our best days, the good things we do are filthy rags before the Lord (Isaiah 64:6). People can do the right things with horrible motives.

Check your motives. Ask, *Why am I doing what I'm doing?*

Real with Others

How can Twos be real with others? They have to declare. What does that mean? It means to say it out loud. Declare that you have needs, and that's okay.

Twos, if you become really unhealthy, you'll become codependent. You won't even exist anymore; you will simply exist to serve someone else. Let me tell you what codependents do; they worship someone other than God. If you become codependent on someone, you are worshipping that person and not God, and that's a sin.

You have to declare that you have needs; you do not exist to serve your children or to serve your spouse. You exist for the glory of God. You were made for Him. You must declare, "I have needs. I can't do it all."

Twos, you can't do it all. And when you try, you make it miserable to be around you. So stop. Take a break. Relax. The laundry will always be there. I have spoken: it will be there; call me a prophet. There will be laundry tomorrow. The house will be dirty tomorrow. Dust will come again. Sometimes you need to take a break. As a Two, you may feel guilty about taking a break. That is shame. Take it to the cross. Twos, why is it you feel guilty about obeying the commandment for a day of rest? Exodus 20:9–10 says, "You have six days each week for your ordinary work, but the seventh day is a Sabbath day of rest dedicated to the LORD your God."

Not long ago, Tammy and I were at dinner with some friends from our church. One of the pastors is a young pastor, and he is still learning to see his wife. She had a baby on one arm, a plate on another arm, and a four-year-old on her leg, and she was trying to make tacos.

I looked at him and said, "Buddy, we've got a problem over here on aisle two!" He said, "Oh yeah, I didn't see that." I said, "Get over there and help."

His wife is a Two. She was probably thinking, *I can do everything. I can have a baby on this arm. I can have a taco plate in this hand. I can have a four-year-old wrestling my leg. I can do it.* No, you can't. It's okay to say, "Can you hold my kids so I can eat?"

I remember coming home from work one time and my kids were standing at the bathroom door, banging on it. "Mom!" My wife was in there. She had locked herself in the bathroom so she could have a moment to herself. We need to pray for all the moms. They can't even pee alone. I told my kids, "Leave her alone. You are not allowed to speak to your mother. Go away."

Twos, learn to ask for help. Say, "I need help." It's okay. This is hard for Twos. They have to learn to confess their sin of pride because people won't see it. People think you are better than everybody else. They say, "Oh, you're always serving, you're always taking part, you're always at church, you're always at the kids' school, you're always at the plays." Yeah, and you're also judging everybody else, and you're self-righteous and prideful. And that sin in you is the Devil. Pride is what made the Devil who he is. Don't be the Devil. Twos, learn to confess it. Learn to say, "My pride got the best of me this week."

Real with God

How can Twos be real with God? They need to learn to declare, "Who I am comes from God's love, not from what I do." The same God does not love me because I'm a pastor; He loves me because I'm His son. And you are His son or daughter if you are in Christ Jesus. You're a child of the King.

God will help you if you ask. Psalm 86:5 says, "O Lord, you are so good, so ready to forgive, so full of unfailing love for all who ask for your help." Twos, God is not going to answer the prayer you don't pray. We worship a God who answers asked prayers.

How Do You Love a Two?

Someone in our church asked a question on our podcast, *The Debrief.* He said, "I'm married to a Two, and I don't know how to love her. We have been married for thirty years." This is why the Enneagram is so important, because you can be married to a person and desperately love a person and not know how to love them. So how do you love a Two?

1. Notice them and thank them for their service.

When you pick up your kids, would you thank the teachers? You know what you dropped off. Some of you don't even go to church for God; you go for a break. Even if I were an atheist, I'd go to church every week. Free childcare? With background-checked and CPR-trained people who love Jesus? Take them. "Wait a minute; these people have to love my kid?" Notice them—and thank them.

2. Ask them what you can do for them.

This is going to be hard for a Two, and they're going to hate you for this, but do it: become an Enneagram ninja. Have them name one thing you can do for them, and watch them squirm. "Can I do a dish? Can I wash a cup? Can I take out the trash?" They're not going to want you to do it. Do you know why? Twos are often not real with themselves. They tend to believe they can do it all, and that's a lie.

3. Help take a night off.

When our kids were little, we were swamped. My wife's days were filled with tears, tantrums, and poopy diapers. So I surprised her with a night out. It was Valentine's Day, so she wasn't that surprised. The surprise was when we came home from dinner, the kids were gone, and the house was silent. I had some friends put rose petals on the stairs all the way up to our bedroom. The truth is, she was tired, and being romantic was the last thing she needed. I could feel her tensing up as we wound up the stairs and entered the bedroom. The bath was drawn, and candles were lit. I told her the bath was for her and her alone. I put a love letter in a bottle next to the bath and asked her to read it, and I left and spent the night with her parents and our screaming-nonstop, pooping children. We have celebrated many Valentine's Days, but the bottle with the love letter inside is the only gift she displays in our house next to our wedding photo. It's a reminder that she had permission as a young mom to have needs and take a night off!

4. Invite them over.

It is important to invite Twos over when you don't need something done. We use Twos. And that's not right.

Whenever we need something done in our house, when my wife needs a honey-do, I call our friend Tim; he's the honey. I say, "Hey, Tim, my wife needs a honey-done. So I need you to come over." The project often involves screws, hammers—man work. And you know what? Tim will always come over. One time when he was at our house, I told him, "Tim, you're my buddy. I love you, and I care for you. You can come over anytime, for no reason. You can come to my house for anything, and we can just sit and have a beer and be men." Which is not actually true; I'm allergic to gluten because God is hilarious. "So Tim, you can have a beer, and I will have a LaCroix, and we will have a very manly conversation about things that I don't understand."

I freaked him out. He said, "We're just gonna sit?" I said, "Well, you'll drink beer, and I'll sit and watch you drink beer. You don't need to do a thing." Tim needs to know that who he is—not what he does—is what matters most to me.

If you really want to mess with a Two, ask them to stop and tell you how their time with God and their family is going. Just ask them, and watch them squirm.

"Tell me about your time with God this week." *Panic.*

"Tell me about your time with the kids." *Panic.*

"Tell me about your time with your husband." *Panic.*

So again, why is a Two afraid of sitting with people? Because of shame. They think, *I'm not good enough.* So they cover that feeling of not being good enough with, "Let me help you." That's not being real.

If you want to begin to be real, you've got to start to share. Twos should share, "My shame is really out of control this week. It's really affecting me. It's tiring to be a Two."

A Prayer for Twos

Here's the prayer of the Twos.

> *God, help me remember that you created me not just for service but for relationships. Help me confess that I can't do it all and learn to ask for help from You and others when I need it.*

Christianity is not a "do" religion. It is spelled done, D-O-N-E. Jesus already did it. Twos, Jesus already did it, so rest in the grace of Jesus. Rest. Here is my prayer for you.

> *Heavenly Father, we love You so much, we love Your grace so much, and we love the Twos. We love the Twos. There's no church without them. And most of our families would unravel and fall apart without the Twos. God, we're grateful for people who want to help, but please help them to know that it's not just their service that we love. We love who they are. You love them, and You care about them, God. They matter more to You than their service. God, help the Twos understand that what You want ultimately is for the Marthas to sit down with the Marys and hear Your Word, because Martha matters just as much to You as Mary. Lord, help us be more like Mary and to sit in Your presence, and help us bring You our shame. We pray this in Jesus' name, amen.*

THE ACHIEVER

Ambition vs. Defeat

Have you ever done something and then said, "Why did I do that? What was I thinking? Why did I think that?" A lot of us don't know why we do what we do. That is what we're trying to uncover in this book. What's driving you? What's motivating you? Why do you do what you do? Why do you do those things that drive you crazy? You don't want the outcome, but you do it anyway. Why do you find yourself there?

In this book, we're using the Enneagram to look at nine personality styles. We started with Ones, the Reformers. They can see the way the world should be, and so, at their best, they make everything better; at their worst, they "should" on themselves, others, and God. Then we looked at Twos, the Helpers. At their best, they serve. They love us. They take care of us. At their worst, they become prideful and resentful because they serve and care for all of us.

In this chapter, we're going to look at Threes, the Achievers. I'm going to try to be delicate because I'm a Three. Just so you know, there are some personality types that if you love one or you know one, you need to wear a helmet. A Three is one of those personality types. If you're married to a Three, you're going to understand why your spirit is sometimes bruised and hurting, because Threes are usually very driven.

My prayer in this chapter is that if you are a Three, you would better understand yourself, and if you know a Three, you would have more compassion for the struggle that is their everyday life.

Threes in the Bible: The Rich Young Ruler

We're going to take a look at a very busy Three. This is what Threes are. They're constantly busy, they're thinking about the future, and they're always in a rush.

In Mark 10:17, the story begins like this: "As Jesus was starting out on his way to Jerusalem, a man came running up to him." Notice that the man is running. Threes are always running. They have places to go. They have things to do. They're going to make stuff happen. Threes feel like life is too short. This is how you know if your child is a Three. Your five-year-old wants to be president of the United States, a pastor, the mayor. A Three wants to be successful at all costs. It's the only thing that matters. At their best, they want to make a difference; at their worst, they just want to look important.

So here's this Three; you may have heard Christians call him "the rich young ruler." This man comes running up to Jesus, kneels down, and says, "Good Teacher, what must I do to inherit eternal life?" Underlying that, here's what he's really asking: "How do I win?" If you have a Three in your life, playing a game with that person is dangerous because the Three wants to win. A Three needs to win, even if they're playing their grandma—she needs to know her place, right?

The Three's mantra is, "If you're not cheating, you're not trying hard enough." To the Three, it's all about the victory. Now, America is the home of the brave and the land of the Three. In America, it's win or die.

How many of you have watched the Super Bowl—even if it's one time? Have you ever seen the team that comes in second and they are all crying? You're like, "Wait a minute. You just played in the Super Bowl. We will never go to the Super Bowl. We can't even afford a ticket to the Super Bowl. And you are crying because you came in second?" And what do Americans do? We cry and quit because it's first or bust. We want to win.

In America, it's not even enough to be a billionaire. We rank them. Did you know that? Every year *Forbes* magazine ranks the wealthiest Americans. And they watch each other. "Oh, you made a billion dollars this year—congratulations. Well, I made ten billion." That's America. You have to be successful. You have to achieve. You have to strive. You have to be the best, no matter what. So Threes feel very at home in America, and they are also very miserable. In this chapter, we'll talk about why.

Back in the book of Mark, the man asked Jesus, "What must I do to inherit eternal life?" (10:17). He was saying, *"Not only am I winning at this life, Jesus, but I want to know how to succeed in the next life too."* So Jesus did a Jedi mind trick where He got to the heart of the issue rather than the question that was asked.

"'Why do you call me good?' Jesus asked. 'Only God is truly

good.' But to answer your question, you know the commandments" (vv. 18–19).

If you don't know the commandments, you might want to review them. They're not called the Ten Suggestions. They're called the Ten Commandments, right? Let's review just a few of them. The fourth one is an excellent place to start: "You must not murder" (Exodus 20:13). If you were thinking about killing somebody this week, God says, *"Don't do that."* Next one: "You must not commit adultery" (v. 14). Some of you don't know what adultery is. It's not that you become an awesome adult. It doesn't mean you've mastered adulthood. What it means is that you cheated on your spouse, or you cheated with someone else's spouse. Don't do that, the Bible says. Next: "You must not steal" (v. 15). Especially if you are a Three, don't steal. Next: "You must not testify falsely against your neighbor" (v. 16). If you're a Three, that's going to be uncomfortable (and it has to do with your core sin, which we'll talk about next). Also: "Honor your father and mother" (v. 12).

"'Teacher,' the man replied. 'I've obeyed all these commandments since I was young'" (Mark 10:20). In other words, *"I've been a Three since I came out of the womb. I have been successful at everything I do."*

"Looking at the man, Jesus felt genuine love for him" (v. 21). And this is interesting for the Three. This is something that's hard for a Three. It's hard for the Three to be real, authentic, and genuine, and notice that Jesus feels genuine love for him. Why does Jesus care about the Three? Because Threes change the world. They drive us crazy, but they change the world. So this man has the potential to change the world.

"There is still one thing you haven't done," Jesus told the man (v. 21). Threes are doing what they have to do to be successful. And

Jesus says there's only one thing they need. Imagine if Jesus just told you the one thing you need to do! Jesus said to the man, "Go and sell all your possessions and give the money to the poor."

Some of you are thinking, *Man, that's easy.* Yeah, that's because you're a college student, and you are broke. I love college students. They say, "Jesus, I'll give You everything. You can have everything in my pocket and my debt. I will follow You." But let's say you've worked hard. Let's say you've made some money. Let's say you bought some homes, you have a portfolio, and you have some retirement. Let's say you've done well in life because you've tried hard. This makes this calling very different. It becomes difficult.

Let's look at the rest of the story: "'Go and sell all your possessions and give the money to the poor, and you will have treasure in heaven. Then come, follow me.' At this, the man's face fell, and he went away sad, for he had many possessions" (v. 21–22). If you're a Three, you don't have possessions; your possessions possess you. This is because Threes tend to define themselves based on the clothes they wear, the car they drive, and the house they live in. The Three is all about image. *"I've got to look successful. I have to seem successful, so everything around me has to make me look good."* If you're a Three, you don't just want a wife; you want a trophy wife, because she's going to make you look good.

Threes are very image conscious. From the time they were little, they cared about the clothes they wore. When I was a kid, I would try to figure out how to put a fake label on my clothes. My heart was Nordstrom, but my mom's budget was Kmart, right? I was like, "Mom, this is killing my style."

Pay attention to this: the rich man thought he had obeyed the commandments perfectly ever since he was a little kid because he was a Three, and he was successful at everything he did. But do you know what the first commandment is? "You must not have any other god but me" (Exodus 20:3). So what did Jesus do? He called out the rich man for worshipping his stuff. Jesus was saying to the rich young ruler, *"Oh, you've mastered all ten? Well, why don't we start with number one."* Now, what's commandment number two? "You must not make for yourself an idol of any kind" (Exodus 20:4). Jesus was saying to the rich man, *"Why don't we really call it out? Why don't you sell everything you have and then come and follow Me? Then you'll have treasure in heaven."*

The Bible says the man's face fell, and he went away sad because he had a lot of stuff. How sad is that? He walked away from ultimate success. If you're a Three, "What do you benefit if you gain the whole world but lose your own soul?" (Mark 8:36). The rich man was going to hell, but he had a lot of stuff.

Threes, when you die, you leave it all. None of it goes with you. The only thing that lasts beyond this life is what you've invested in heaven, Jesus said. So, Jesus told this rich man, "Give all that you have, and you'll have treasure in heaven." Jesus also said, "Wherever your treasure is, there the desires of your heart will also be" (Matthew 6:21).

Let's get back to our story about the rich young man. "Then Jesus said to his disciples, 'I tell you the truth, it is very hard for a rich person to enter the Kingdom of Heaven!'" (Matthew 19:23). In the ancient world, everybody thought if you were rich, you were blessed. If you're rich, God loves you. If you're rich in this life, they thought, surely you'll be rich in the next life. Jesus completely flipped that idea upside down. Jesus said not only is it hard for the rich to get into heaven, but it is impossible for them to do so. "Jesus said again, 'Dear children, it is very hard to enter the Kingdom of God. In fact, it is easier for a camel to go through the eye of a needle than for a rich person to enter the Kingdom of God!'" (Mark 10:24–25). You may be asking, "What on earth does that mean?" Let me be honest with you. No one knows exactly what that means.

But Jesus told us what it meant. It means it is impossible. You can't get to heaven on your own—even if you're loaded. The disciples were astounded. They asked, "Then who in the world can be saved?" (v. 26). I love this next part. "Jesus looked at them intently" (v. 27). Remember this next time you and I talk. People are always intimidated when I talk to them. My kids say, "Dad, you can't stare into people's souls when you talk." I'm an intense talker; that's how God made me. Why? Because I wanna be like Jesus. Jesus looked at them intently. As I mentioned, I have ADD, so if I don't look at your face, I can't hear your words. I look intently at people, and they're like, "Oh, this is weird." I've only met one person in the world who talks like I do: Vice President Mike Pence. He stared into my soul. I stared back because I'm a Three; I have to win. We had a stare down in the White House. It was awkward, but it really happened. My wife was like, "Look away," and I said, "I can't; I'm a Three."

"Jesus looked at them intently and said, 'Humanly speaking, it is impossible'" (v. 27). Many of you don't believe this. You don't believe that it's impossible for you to earn your way to heaven. You know why I know you don't believe this? Because you don't share your faith. You don't share your faith in Christ with your Hindu friends, with your Muslim friends, with your atheist friends. You don't share your faith in Christ with your friends who believe they're good enough to get in heaven on their own. You don't share your faith because you believe that there's some way other than Jesus for people to get to heaven. A lot of people believe that.

People tell me all the time, "Well, I believe I'm a good person, so I'll get into heaven." Do you know what the problem with that is? When people believe that, they're comparing themselves to the other ignorant people they know. They're thinking, *I'm pretty good. Look at them. I'm not as bad as they are.* Well, show me the verse in the Bible where it says they're the standard.

A couple of years ago, I was getting ready to do my first Ironman event. If you don't know what that is, it's an event for crazy people. Seriously, you swim 2.4 miles, you ride your bike 112 miles, and you run a marathon in one day. And you have to do it in less than sixteen hours, or you're disqualified. So a sweet lady in our church came up to me, and she said, "Pastor, I'm praying for you and your Ironman this week. I hope you win."

I said, "What do you mean? You hope I win?"

She says, "Well, don't you think you're going to win?"

I said, "No."

She said, "Well, you're the fittest person I know."

I said, "But I'm not racing you." So that's why my church no longer lets me do counseling.

You know why you're not going to go to heaven apart from Jesus? Because you're not Jesus. You're not getting in. Your friends aren't getting in. Your family is not getting in. Gandhi is not getting in. Mother Teresa is not getting in. Billy Graham is not getting in. The pope is not getting in. No one is getting in unless they follow Jesus. He's the only way. It's impossible. You can't get to heaven from here apart from Jesus.

That is why we need to share our faith. That is why we need to tell people about Jesus. Even the most successful people, even Threes, even the rich young ruler who had tried to do everything right since he was a kid can't get there from here. Jesus said, "Humanly speaking, it is impossible. But with God everything is possible" (v. 27).

The Character of Threes: They Reflect God's Hope

Threes are Achievers, and they reflect God's hope. Here's what makes the Three unique. The beauty of Ones is that they see how, if you just tweak something, it could be better. Ones can make things better. They can adjust. Twos can serve and make sure that our needs are taken care of and we feel loved and we feel cared for. That's the beauty of the Ones and Twos. But Threes don't adjust, and they certainly don't serve.

Here's the beauty of the Three: They are not limited to what we see in the world. Threes see things that aren't.

Not long ago, Tammy and I went to Washington, DC. And if you're married, take notes; here's how you enjoy vacations as a married couple. You say, "Honey, what would you like to do?" And then hopefully she'll ask what you would like to do and then you both get to do what you want to do. We launched into that discussion about our hopes for DC.

Okay, so in DC, you can't do everything; there's just not enough time. My wife really wanted to see the Hope Diamond. Now, for a Three, that's torture. Why? Because you can't buy it. You can't afford it. You will never make enough money. The Hope Diamond is worth $350 million, and it's locked up and guarded by guards, so you can't get it. So for a Three, that's like a nightmare. *Oh, look at this thing I'll never own.* My wife said, "What's the one thing you want to see?" The one thing I wanted to see was the airplane the Wright brothers built.

You may not know this, but your life has been affected by these two brothers—who, by the way, were bicycle mechanics. At the time it was believed that human flight was impossible, but these two brothers saw something that didn't exist. That's what Threes do. They see things that don't exist. They see things that nobody else sees, and they go for what the world says is impossible. The Smithsonian's National Air and Space Museum website highlights this quote from a 1906 *New York Herald* article: "The Wrights have flown or they have not flown. They possess a machine or they do not possess one. They are in fact either fliers or liars. It is difficult to fly. It is easy to say, 'We have flown.'"[1] How many of you have been on an airplane? They were fliers.

Threes reflect hope. They see something that no one else sees.

The Core Motivation of Threes: Success

What drives Threes? What's the core motivation of their hearts? One word: *success*. They have to be successful. If you've got a first grader who wants to buy a suit, chances are that he's a Three. *I've got to be successful. I've got to be a big deal.* It doesn't matter what it is. They have to be the best. They sell real estate. They have to sell more than you. They drive a nicer car. They're going to have a better-looking spouse and better-looking kids who are better dressed. It doesn't matter what the game is. The Three has to win, and you have to lose.

The Three's motivation is to be successful. It can be academics, it can be money, it can be acting, performing, singing, or dancing. Threes don't care what the stage is as long as they're on the stage, right? And as long as you're in the audience, appreciating their glory. And that's coming from a Three who is on stage almost every day.

Threes Need to Achieve

What's the deep underlying need of Threes? Their need is to achieve.

Threes want to leave their mark. They want to be remembered. And for some of you, that seems crazy. Why do they care so much about what people think? Because that's what the Three cares about. They want to be read about and remembered. They want to make a difference. They want to see their names in lights. They want to be popular. They want to be wealthy. They want to be famous. They've got to achieve.

Threes Focus on Goals

Where do Threes direct their intensity? Now, if you love a Three, pay attention: they focus on goals.

Here's the thing: if you love a Three, don't believe their goals. Their goals are always moving. A Three will lie to you. They'll say, "My goal is to get my PhD," and then when they get it, they will now get another because they have to have the most PhDs of anyone on earth ever. A Three will say, "Once I make a million dollars, I'll be satisfied." Then one million is ten million, then ten million is one hundred million, then one hundred million is a billion, and then a billion is a trillion. Don't believe their goals. If Threes are unhealthy, they will never be satisfied. They're insatiable. Their goals are a moving target. But they're focused on the things they're going to do with their lives.

The Core Sin of Threes: Lying

Here's the core sin of a Three: lying. They're not always honest. Do you know why? Because the truth is painful.

Threes have such a need to be successful that they have to create lies to meet their standards. Isn't that crazy? Threes are some of the most successful people we know. Many of you look up to Threes, listen to Threes, and follow Threes. Your lives have been changed by Threes. But they're so insecure in who they are. They lie about their accomplishments because they feel like no matter what they accomplish, it's never enough. So they lie to everybody, including themselves. Why? Because they need to avoid failure.

Threes Avoid Failure

Threes, we don't fail. We don't lose; we just run out of time. We can't fail—we just *can't*. Failure is not an option.

I didn't know this, but a lot of people have panic attacks during the swim of their first Ironman event. Why? Because you put yourself in the water with a bunch of other unhealthy Threes. There are three thousand other people competing with you, and they shoot off a gun, and everybody tries to win. What that means is you're going to get pushed underwater. I'm not super big, so I got pushed underwater a lot, and I felt like I was going to drown. I swam over in the first one hundred yards and found a boat. What I didn't know is that the Boy Scouts and Girl Scouts try to earn a badge that week by helping rescue any swimmers in need. So I swam over to the boat to be rescued, and I put my hand on the boat, which is legal for a time. The boat can't carry you, but it can save you. I put a hand on the boat and looked up, and I saw a Girl Scout with her vest on. I thought, *I would rather die*, and I just let go. I remember thinking, *I am not going to be saved by a Girl Scout. That is not going to happen. They can sell me cookies, but they cannot save my life. I didn't fail. I died trying.* How sick is that? I would rather my wife be a widow and my children become orphans than receive help from a Girl Scout earning a badge? But that's how strongly I avoid failure. I cannot fail.

If you're a Three, do you know what failure does? It deepens and strengthens you. But Threes are shallow. We run from the things we can't win at. Do you know how you become a more profound person? By embracing failure and learning from failure. You can't do it all. So Threes are the most driven people on earth.

But here's the reality. Threes, there is a limit to your ability, despite what America says to you. The dumbest thing we tell kids, especially Threes, is that they can be anything they want. Anyone who has ever looked at my skinny, short body knows I cannot be an NBA basketball player. Genetically, it's not in the cards. What if I told you I wanted to be a linebacker? Steroids aren't going to help with that. I'd be in one play, then *pow!* I'm dead.

Threes, you're going to run into people who are more successful than you are. If you're unhealthy, you will never be okay with that. No matter how much money you have, someone has more. No matter how good looking you are, there's always somebody better looking. One hundred years ago, you could fool yourself and be the best-looking person in your town. Now, there's the Internet, and you can see and compare yourself to everybody else. You could have been the richest person in your city, but now there's *Forbes* magazine, and you didn't even make the list. They don't even know you exist. You have to embrace that.

Threes Fear Being Worthless

For Threes, their greatest fear is all about being worthless. They think, *If I don't have nice clothes, who am I? If I don't drive the best car, who am I?* When Tammy and I first got married, our car payment was more than our house payment. Yeah, I'm an idiot. Not only did I get a dog, I got a big dog—bigger than your dog. I didn't have the money to feed the big dog, but it didn't matter; I'm a Three. My dog will eat your dog. It's crazy. What was I doing with my life? Here's what I was doing: I was all about the image. Why? Because the underlying emotion of the Three is shame.

If my underlying emotion is shame, I think, *If I don't have my clothes, you won't love me. If I don't drive this car, you won't date me. If I don't have this house, you won't come over. If I'm not successful, you won't care about me. I won't matter to you.* The fear of the Three is this: *If you really knew me, you wouldn't love me, you wouldn't want to be my friend, you wouldn't celebrate me.* This is why so many actors in Hollywood go crazy—because they're Threes. And here's what they believe: *Once I become famous, I'll be satisfied.* Then they become famous, and they're miserable.

I've followed the career of the comedian and actor Jim Carrey, and one thing he's famously said is, "I think everybody should get rich and famous and do everything they ever dreamed of so they can see that it's not the answer." The problem is that Threes don't listen to that. They believe the lie.

No amount of success can ever cover your shame. Only the blood of Jesus can. Threes, don't chase your dreams; chase the cross. Run to the cross, because only the cross can deal with what is wrong inside you.

How Threes Can Be Real with Self, Others, and God

So how on earth does a Three get real?

Real with Self

Threes need to be real with themselves. Psalm 119:29 says, "Keep me from lying to myself." If you're a Three, you lie to yourself more than anybody else. You're not honest about how you feel, what you've done, and where you're going. The psalmist continued, "Keep me from lying to myself; give me the privilege of knowing your instructions." You see, Ones have an internal moral compass. They know what's right. But Threes have no compass, so they need God's instructions.

If you're a Three, you have to drive, but you don't have a steering wheel. God's Word is the steering wheel to control where you take that drive. Without God's Word, you're going to be lost, and you're going to destroy yourself. If you're a Three, your dream may be your nightmare. It may be the very thing God came to save you from. That's why I hate when people go to these churches where they hear sermons about how God came to fulfill your dreams. When I read God's Word, much of what God's doing is trying to save us from our dreams.

Some of you have got what you always wanted. So how is it? It's a mess. If you're a Three, facts are your friends. Never stray from the facts. You can lie to yourself for a time, but "Jesus said to the people who believed in him, 'You are truly my disciples if you remain faithful to my teachings. And you will know the truth, and the truth will set you free'" (John 8:31–32).

Real with Others

How can Threes be real with others? James 5:16 says, "Confess your sins to each other and pray for each other so that you may be healed." Confession is your friend. You have to learn to tell people, "Yeah, you know that story I told, that's not true. That's not what happened. Here's what really happened."

James 5:16 continues, "The earnest prayer of a righteous person has great power and produces wonderful results." Threes, do you want your prayer life to change? You need to change and start confessing. I remember the first time I got real. The first time I looked someone in the eye and told them the truth. Honestly, it was terrifying—and it has been every time I've done it since. Just recently, while my wife was away on a trip, I was looking at different vacation spots in Hawaii for us to go to. While looking at photos on Instagram, I stumbled across a beautiful beach I had never been to before. Three clicks later I was looking at a picture of an athletic female model in her newest swimsuit posing on that beach. So I looked at a couple more photos, felt terrible, and went to bed. A few days later, I was so glad when Tammy got back in town, but I had forgotten about my little eye vacation on Instagram.

Later that night when we were in bed, as Tammy leaned over to kiss me goodnight, she paused and asked who so-and-so was. I said who? She said, "That swimsuit model. You liked three of her pictures!" I looked my wife straight in the face and said, "I have no idea what you're talking about." She said okay, kissed me, and went to bed.

She slept like and angel, but I couldn't sleep a wink. I couldn't believe I could still lie like that. After all, I am pastor who planted a church that's all about being real. I couldn't wait for the sun to come up. As soon as it did, I confessed. It was terrifying but not as scary as slipping back in to the old lies I had struggled with. The only hope for you as a Three is that you fear lying and its power over you more than consequences of telling the truth. Tammy was gracious, and she reminds me again and again of how blessed I am to have someone who loves me not for what I do but for who I am.

Real with God

How can Threes be real with God? In 1 Samuel 16:7, God said to Samuel, "Don't judge by his appearance or height, for I have rejected him." And some of you don't know the story, but here's the issue.

Israel had a king named Saul, but Saul blew it. Israel needed a new king, so God called His prophet Samuel, and he said, "*I want you to go to the house of Jesse. Jesse has a bunch of sons.*" Statistically, having more than twelve boys is a miracle in itself. Jesse had all these sons. So Samuel went to Jesse's house, and Jesse lined his sons up from the oldest to the youngest, from the tallest to the shortest. God cautioned Samuel, "*Don't you dare look at how they appear.*"

God says, "*I don't give a rip how you look on the outside. I care about who you are on the inside.*" Samuel asked Jesse, "Are these all the sons you have?" Jesse said, "There is still the youngest. But he's out in the fields watching the sheep and goats" (v. 11). In other words, "*Little David? Yes, little David—he's out in the fields. I didn't think God would be interested in him.*" That's the very son God chose to be the king of Israel.

The Lord does not see things the way you or I see them. People judge by outward appearance, especially Threes. But the Lord looks at the heart. That's where the Three doesn't want to go because of shame. For a Three, the work you need to do is almost never about anything on the outside. The work is on the inside. None of your accomplishments or exaggerated stories can cover the shame you feel deep down inside. There will always be someone younger, richer, or more successful than you. But there will never be anyone who loves you more than God. Psalm 145:18 says that the Lord is near to all those who call upon Him in truth. Learn to get real with God, yourself, and others. Make that a success so you can experience what the next verse says—that God will fulfill your desires. Threes, the fastest way to success is God; just be prepared for Him to change your view of success.

How Do You Love a Three?

So how on earth do you love a Three? With a helmet. Be careful.

1. Encourage them to celebrate success.

Do you know why that is? Threes are so forward-thinking they can't ever celebrate what God did. This week, my wife and I had a quick conversation. She was holding all my Ironman medals. Do you know what I told her? "Throw those away."

She said, "I'm not going to throw these away. We're going to mount them on the wall."

I was like, "Why would you do that?"

She said, "Because they're a big deal."

Threes are terrible at celebrating success. Here's why you need to celebrate: because it reminds the Three of what God did. In the Old Testament, this is called an Ebenezer. They put up a big stone of remembrance so they could remember what God did. Threes are so focused on the future that they can screw up the present.

A Three is so goal-oriented that they'll miss a birthday party. You must tell your kids they matter, and you will be there. You see, a Three will change the world and lose their family. You hear about a lot of these great people who did amazing things, and they were terrible spouses and worse parents. Listen to me, Threes: who you are is who you are in the home.

2. Be real with them.

It's hard; Threes are overwhelming. They are big personalities. They are tough to compete with. You've got to be real with them. Pay attention to this, Threes. What good is it if you inherit the whole world, but you lose your soul, you lose your family, you lose your friends? As a Three, you can be the most popular person in the world, you can have one hundred thousand followers on Twitter and not have any real friends. You see, as a Three, you can be the most popular and the loneliest because you're fake; you are not real. Does anybody wonder why God would call me to plant a church whose vision was to be real with self, God, and others? It's because that's the kind of church I needed. If you are a Three, you need a church like that too.

3. Accept that they are a little nuts.

They're a little off. Can you imagine if you were the mother of the Wright brothers?

"Boys, what are you going to do with your lives?"

"We're going to fly!"

"Like a bird?"

"Yes."

"That's nuts! If God wanted you to fly, He would have given you wings."

"Well, we're going to make our own wings."

Threes are just a little skewed. They tend to do things that don't make sense—like use their vacation time to do Ironmans. For most normal people, vacation involves an umbrella and an iced drink. For a Three, it involves suffering and vomiting.

4. Encourage them to connect with how they're feeling.

Do you know why? They don't deal with the heart. That's scary. Tammy and I went to counseling a year and a half ago because she was struggling. I was convinced God was going to do something amazing in her life. We went to three days of counseling with two counselors eight hours a day. Tammy was sharing her story, and I was waiting for God to move because I wanted to be successful, right? The counselors would periodically stop looking at her and look at me. They would ask this question: "How are you feeling?" And I would say, "This is great." Later they asked again, "How are you feeling?" Day two, hour four, I started getting an eye twitch. So I responded, "Why do you keep asking me that?"

The counseling was not having a big impact on Tammy, so I was getting a little frustrated. Tammy and I went to lunch, I ordered a salad, and all I remember is I started crying.

"What is this?" I asked.

"Those are feelings," she pointed out.

For the rest of the time, the counseling focused on me. I asked the counselor, "Why do you keep asking me questions? We're here for her."

He said, "You're a Three, so you don't know how you feel." He said, "You're completely disconnected from your feelings. You're so focused on being successful that you can't deal with the emotional failure and pain in your life." Threes, you have to connect with your heart. Threes are scared to death of their feelings because they don't always work out successfully.

5. Thank them specifically.

Say, "I appreciate your hard work in this. I appreciate that you do this." Make them pause and let them know that you appreciate not just what they do, but you appreciate them. Because what do Threes fear? They fear that they don't matter to you; all that matters is what they do for you. That's the Three's relational fear. Threes think, *If I'm no longer able to produce the money I make, to provide the lifestyle we live, no one will love me.* So you've got to reassure the

Three that you do. You can tell a Three, "We love you, not just the lifestyle you provide or the entertainment that you give. You're more than what you do."

A Prayer for Threes

Here's the prayer of the Three:

God, help me find success in You. Help me strive for obedience as I strive for success.

I love this verse: "May integrity and honesty protect me, for I put my hope in you" (Psalm 25:21).

If you're a Three, you're beautiful, and you're a gift to the church. Your integrity must match your intensity. You must close the gap between your calling and your character. It is a lifelong struggle, because as a Three, you will do great things for God or for the Devil, your choice. My prayer is that you choose to do great things for God.

Heavenly Father, we thank You for Threes. We love them, Lord. They change our lives, they make such incredible differences in the world, and they see things we don't see. God, I pray as they pursue success that they would have a heart to pursue You over and above everything else. Let them seek obedience, and match their integrity with their ability. We pray this in Jesus' name, amen.

THE INDIVIDUALIST

Uniqueness vs. Envy

When I first encountered the Enneagram about fifteen years ago, it transformed my life. It changed the way I see God because it changed the way I see myself. It made me a better dad, and it made me a better husband. It made me a better Christian and a better pastor. I believe that if you take the time to get to know yourself and let God speak, He will transform and change your life.

In this chapter we are talking about the Four, the Individualist. If you are a parent raising a little Four, I beg you to read this chapter over and over again. Because if you're raising a Four, you might want to jump off a cliff. Don't do that, because Fours are special, they're unique, and they're amazing. And don't you dare change them. That's the way God made them. They're almost always misunderstood.

If you are a Four, don't panic. If you know your Bible, you're going to freak out when I tell you who we're going to talk about as a biblical example of a Four. I think the person we're going to talk about in this chapter gets a bad rap. He was an amazing individual who was thrust into an incredible position of leadership, and it was excruciatingly difficult for him. Because of his obedience to God, this person transformed and changed the nation of Israel.

If you're a Four, pay attention, because God has a beautiful plan for your life. He made you. Don't ever, ever let somebody tell you that you need to be different. Be who God called you to be. As they say, everybody else is already taken.

In the previous chapter, we talked about the Three. America is the home of the brave and the land of the Three. In America, we love Threes, but we squash Fours; that's what we do. We eat them up, we spit them out, but we need them. They're amazing. If there are no Fours in your church or community group, get one, because they feel the heart of God. They feel your feelings, especially if you're a Three. You need a Four so you can discover your emotions. They know your feelings better than you do, and they're awesome.

Fours in the Bible: King Saul

In this chapter, we are going to talk about King Saul. He was an amazing individual. Most of you know his story because it ends in a cloud of dust, some emotional rants, and throwing spears at people. But there was so much more to the man, so let's take a look at 1 Samuel.

If you're new to Christianity, you should read the two books of 1 and 2 Samuel. They are amazing, amazing books. Samuel is one of the most important characters in the entire history of our faith. You need to know about him. Samuel led Israel for a period of time.

In 1 Samuel 16, Samuel is at the end of his life, and he's not doing well. He was a tremendous leader but not a great dad. Many leaders are not great dads. So Samuel raised some knucklehead sons, and Israel was freaking out: *"We love Samuel, but his boys make us nervous. We want a king. We don't want Samuel's family line."* Samuel was upset about it. He went to the Lord, and the Lord said, basically, *"Give the people what they want."* Be careful; if you keep asking God for stuff, He might give it to you. God said, *"Fine. Enough. Give them what they want. They want a king? They can have a king."*

Here's the story: "Samuel called all the people of Israel to meet before the LORD at Mizpah" (1 Samuel 10:17). Look at that word *Mizpah*, because this is important. In the book of Judges, something else happens at Mizpah—that's where the extermination of the tribe of Benjamin almost takes place. The other eleven tribes of Israel gathered at Mizpah because the tribe of Benjamin was wicked and evil. They set out to wipe them off the face of the earth at Mizpah. Remember the tribe of Benjamin. Just put that in your noodle, and let it sit there. We'll get to it in a bit.

Samuel said to the people of Israel, "This is what the LORD, the God of Israel, has declared" (v. 18). Okay, this is God. He said, "I brought you from Egypt and rescued you from the Egyptians and from all of the nations that were oppressing you. But though I have rescued you from your misery and distress, you have rejected your God today and have said, 'No, we want a king instead!'" (vv. 18–19). This is what God's people do; we want to be led by our own emotions, our own desires, and not God. God says, *"Fine. You want a king? I'll give you a king."* We say, *"But I'm supposed to be the king."* If you don't know this already, Jesus is supposed to be your King, so get off the throne. There are not two seats. There's not one there for you; it's for Jesus. Samuel said to the people, "You have rejected your God today and have said, 'No, we want a king instead!' Now, therefore, present yourselves before the LORD by tribes and by clans" (v. 19).

In the nation of Israel, your tribe is your big group; that's who you are. There are twelve tribes in the nation of Israel, and within those twelve tribes, there are clans. God was saying, "*I want you all to appear before Me.*" Notice that God did not say, "*Today we're going to pick from all of your tribes and your clans, and we are going to elect a king.*" Instead, God says, "*I've chosen the king.*" And God chose a Four to be the King. If you're a Four, the world will never realize how special you are, but God does. God sees you for who you are.

"So Samuel brought all the tribes of Israel before the LORD, and the tribe of Benjamin was chosen by lot" (v. 20). What does that mean? Did they gamble, throw some dice, and just see what happened? No. God was in control. He is in control, but we're always freaking out, right? Obama gets elected: "Oh my gosh." Trump gets elected: "Oh my gosh." Everybody's freaking out. God is not surprised. God is not sitting in heaven watching cable news and saying, "*I wonder who will get elected today? Jesus, how do You think this is going to turn out?*" They're not up in heaven, eating popcorn, wondering what's going to happen. God knows. He's in control. He understands exactly what's happening.

The people in Israel realized, *Okay, God's going to choose somebody to be our king.* So they brought forth each family of the tribe of Benjamin. Remember, they had gathered at Mizpah at one time to exterminate the tribe of Benjamin, but they didn't do it. The tribe of Benjamin is still here. Notice, Fours, that the tribe of Benjamin is the smallest, most insignificant tribe, yet the most significant person will come from that tribe. "Then he brought each family of the tribe of Benjamin before the LORD, and the family of the

Matrites was chosen. And finally Saul son of Kish was chosen from among them" (v. 21). The people were excited. *"We know who the new king is. We now have a leader!"* But when they looked for him, he had disappeared. Why does a Four do that? A Four says, "I'm in the spotlight, so I'm out of here." There was one person in the crowd who didn't want to be king. He didn't want to be thrown in front of everybody. "So they asked the LORD, 'Where is he?'" (v. 22). They just got a new king, and they can't find him.

I love this. If you're a Four, you can hide from people, but you can't hide from God. "The LORD replied, 'He's hiding among the baggage'" (v. 22). He's right over there. Some of you think, *I'll run from God. I'll go to Vegas. I'll move to California. I'll move away from California. I'll go wherever I want to go.* God will find you.

When I ran from God, I joined the United States Army. I ran from Him: *No, I will not serve you, God. I will serve America.* I joined the army. Do you know what they did the first weekend at boot camp? They made us go to church. It was a different time. I was awakened at 4:00 a.m. with a trash can. *Bam! Bam! Bam! Bam!* "Get up, Brown." You know what my drill sergeant told me? He said, "You have a problem. You know what the problem is, Private Brown?"

I said, "No, sir."

He said, "Your name is too dang easy to remember." So when he didn't know who to yell at, guess who he picked? "Private Brown, get over here." Do you know what he told me? He said, "You're going to church today."

I said, "I don't want to go to church."

He said, "I don't care. Get up. You're going to church."

I tried running from God. But you can't run from God. God said, *"Where's Matt? Where's Private Brown? There he is in the baggage. Get him*—bam! *He's going to church.*" Do you know what happened? I went to church. I cried for the whole service, right there in front of fellow soldiers. Do you know why? Because I have some Four in me. It's one of the major influences in my life.

I cry all the time. I've seen *The Notebook* a thousand times, and I cry every time. As I said in Type Two, my wife and kids, they don't watch the movie; they watch me. "You crying again, Dad? You know, she doesn't know who he is." Me, crying, "It's just so good . . ." I'm just emotional. I have a lot of Four in me.

The people of Israel asked where Saul was, and the Lord replied, "He's hiding among the baggage." The story continues, "So they found him and brought him out, and he stood head and shoulders above everyone else" (v. 23). And if you're a Four, you always will. Do you know why? If you're a Four, people are critical of you because they're envious of you and your gift, your uniqueness, your talent. You're different. You don't look like everybody else. You don't act like everybody else. And so often what we do in our culture when someone is a little different is we try to wreck them.

Why would it be significant that the Lord would say that Saul stood head and shoulders above everyone else? Because if you're a Jew, you're God's chosen people; but in general, you're kind of short. Saul was taller than everybody else. When you read the Bible, usually when the Israelites described the enemies of God, they said, "*They are really, really tall.*" Because as a Jew, that was important information. "*We are fighting tall guys.*" It's like on a basketball team. If you are short, you're going to lose. It's not good. Thank God that the Jews had God, amen?

Saul was taller than everyone else. "Then Samuel said to all the people, 'This is the man the LORD has chosen as your king. No one in all Israel is like him!'" (v. 24). If you're a Four, stop apologizing for being different. Stop apologizing for feeling different. God has made you different. *No one is like him.*

"And all the people shouted, 'Long live the king!'" (v. 24). When you read the next chapter, it says not everybody liked Saul, not everybody agreed with him. Welcome to leadership. Read the next chapter in the book of Judges. Some people didn't bless him, did not honor him, didn't like him. Why? Because he was a little different. *"Why was Saul hiding in the baggage? Because as a Four, Saul could only see his baggage, but the Lord saw through the baggage, and He can see through yours. Fours can usually only see disaster, but God can see your potential."*

The Character of Fours: They Reflect God's Uniqueness

Let's talk about the Four. Fours reflect God's uniqueness. God is unique. He said to Moses, "There is no one like me in all the earth" (Exodus 9:14). He was saying, *"Moses, I'm going to send you to Pharaoh, who believes that all gods are the same; all religions lead to the same place. But there is no one like Me in all the earth, and don't you ever let Pharaoh forget it."*

Who picks a stutterer to proclaim their message? God does. Exodus 4:10 says Moses was "slow of speech and of tongue" (NIV). That means he stuttered. That's who God picked to announce his glory. Do you know why? Because it wasn't about Moses' words; it was about the power of God. The Four reflects God's distinct nature. If you're a Four, you understand why Moses said, *"God, I can't talk. You picked the wrong one, God. You never should have picked me."* Fours never feel like they're supposed to lead. Yet often, they're the only ones who can feel and sense the direction of God. Everybody else is going their own way. But Fours say, "I don't feel like we should be doing this. This doesn't feel right." They reflect the uniqueness of God.

The Core Motivation of Fours: Significance

Now here's what's amazing. Threes wants to be successful. They don't care how they feel; they just want to win at your expense, right? They want to win, and they need you to lose so everybody knows where everybody sits on the food chain. Fours don't want to win, but they want to feel like what they're doing matters. So if you're raising a Four, they're not going to be interested in making a lot of money. They're going to be interested in doing something that matters. You'll send your Four to college and spend two hundred thousand dollars, and they'll pick a career path. They'll earn ten bucks an hour, but it's something that makes a difference. You're pulling your hair out as a Three because your little Four wants to do something that matters. That's who they are. They care about making an impact. Fours want their lives to matter. So their core motivation is significance.

Here's one of the things that is amazing about the Bible. When a king dies, the Jews who write about the king are brutally honest. You don't want to be a Jewish king because if you sucked as a king, they would let everybody know. They'll say, "*You were terrible. You were so terrible that you don't get to be buried with the kings. We don't even like you. We didn't like you when you were alive, and we don't like you now that you are dead.*" Jews are very real about their leaders.

But when you read in 1 Samuel 14 about Saul, the people loved him. It says this: "Now when Saul had secured his grasp on Israel's throne, he fought against his enemies in every direction—against Moab, Ammon, Edom, the kings of Zobah, and the Philistines. And wherever he turned, he was victorious. He performed great deeds and conquered the Amalekites, saving Israel from all those who had plundered them" (vv. 47–48). Have you ever seen where Israel is situated on the map? It's right in the middle of every significant superpower for the last three thousand years. Their enemies are in every direction. America has been blessed in that we are separated by vast amounts of water, right? We have the Atlantic Ocean, and we have the Pacific Ocean, so we've been very safe. Israel is not so secure. So what did Saul do as king? He fought against his enemies in every direction, and he performed great deeds, saving Israel from their enemies. That's pretty astounding.

You can control what you do in life. You can't control what people say about you when you die; people can say what they want. They are at your funeral and eating potato salad. You paid for it. You're dead. They're going to say whatever they want to say. One time I went to a funeral, and there was an old lady who had to be in her nineties. We buried her husband. I asked, "How are you doing?"

She said, "I'm just glad he's gone."

Then she said, "The potato salad is good."

Wow.

See, when you're dead, people tell the truth about you. The truth is that Saul was an amazing leader.

Fours Need Uniqueness

What's the core inner need of Fours? If you are a Four, you need to be unique. And if you're a Four, you are unique.

Fours Focus on What's Missing

What is a Four's focus? What's missing. This is literally the thorn in the Four's flesh. Fours have a hard time being happy because they're constantly focused on what's missing, what's wrong with the world, what's wrong with their clothes, what's wrong with their status. They can be overwhelmed with what's missing. They struggle being satisfied. If they're not careful, Fours can really enjoy being depressed and kind of dark.

And if you know the story of King Saul, it gets a little dark. He gets depressed. As a matter of fact, they had to bring in a young guy by the name of David to play the harp to soothe King Saul when he was feeling really, really emotionally low.

The Core Sin of Fours: Envy

What's the core sin of the Four? If you are a Four, get off Instagram; it's Envy-a-gram for you. Get off it; don't look at it. There's going to be somebody else more creative on it. You'll think, *I should have thought of that*, or *I've had that idea in my mind forever*. Don't linger there. This is the madness of our modern society. Every idea, every unique thing you have, there's somebody else who is doing it. The core sin of the Four is envy.

Fours want to be the most unique, the most special. If someone else is unique and special, that's threatening to Fours. They want to be the only weird one. But have you looked around? Have you noticed there are some other Fours? But they are thinking, *I need to be the only one who is creative, who's an individual, and there can be no one even remotely like me because then I have to hate them.*

Guess what happened in King Saul's life? He became so

preoccupied with David that he completely lost sight of who he was. Here's what happens in 1 Samuel 18:7–9. Young King David is being raised up, and David is a warrior. David's amazing, right? The story isn't that Saul defeats Goliath. Remember, the story is that David defeats Goliath. So people started to get excited about the newer, younger, fresher version of Saul.

The women started singing this song: "Saul has killed his thousands, and David his ten thousands!" (v. 7). Ooh, that hit a sore spot. "This made Saul very angry. 'What is this?' he said. 'They credit David with ten thousands and me with only thousands. Next they'll be making him their king!' So from that time on Saul kept a jealous eye on David" (vv. 8–9). Do you know where Saul's eyes should have been? On God. If you're a Four and you're Saul, when God chooses David to be king, you need to listen to His words. Samuel said to King Saul: "The LORD has sought out a man after his own heart" (1 Samuel 13:14).

If you're a Four, you can be overwhelmed with your heart, your emotions, your feelings, and you can be so consumed with how you feel that you lose your faith. If you've read the Bible, David isn't perfect; wait until we get to type Seven. We're going to study David. David likes to party, right? Sometimes it's with Bathsheba. Sometimes it's naked, worshipping God. That's a little strange. That's the Seven; they like parties.

So, "Saul kept a jealous eye on David" (1 Samuel 18:9). What's the underlying emotion? We're still in the shame quadrant. Twos, Threes, and Fours feel shame. If you're a Two, you're ashamed that you're not good enough unless you're doing something to help. You have got to serve somebody. If you're a Three, you're ashamed that you're not good enough, so you wrap yourself in things or in achievement. If you're a Four, you're ashamed of being ordinary. You're not special. You're not unique. And what's tragic is that if you're a Four, you are unique. There are fewer Fours than any other number in America. You're automatically unique and special by merely being a Four. You are not ordinary. It's a lie; don't believe it.

Remember what God said to Eve: "Who told you that you were naked?" (Genesis 3:11). If you're a Four, here's what you need to hear from God: "*Who told you that you are ordinary?*" Because it's not God. God knows you're special, and God sees you. God saw Saul. He picked him from the crowd, and when Saul tried to run from his creative destiny, God said, "*He's in the baggage. I see him. You can't run from Me. You didn't think I noticed, but I noticed because I'm God. So get over here and let us anoint you as king.*"

I want to go back to the summary of Saul's death. Notice the Bible doesn't say the people hated Saul. They loved him. Saul fought Israel's enemies in every direction. He protected them, he was valiant, and he was loyal to them. The nation grieved when Saul died. You may not know this, but when God anointed David king, there was a civil war that raged in Israel for thirty years. Do you know why? Because people were still loyal to the line of Saul. They loved Saul, and they remained true to him.

Fours Avoid Being Basic

What does the Four avoid? Being basic. You're not taking your Four kids to the department store. They are going to make their clothes, right? The Three wants a label. The Four hates a label. They're going to find some reason they want to be different. They'll say, "If you were really in touch with your feelings, you would have sewn your clothes yourself from materials you got on a spiritual trip to India." I don't have that much Four. I don't need to sew my clothing and weave it from some hair from a camel somewhere in India. I don't need to do that, but Fours do that, and that's just fantastic.

Fours Fear Being Unnoticed

What is the Four's main fear? Being unnoticed.

Often, if you have multiple children, the middle child is the most likely to be a Four. They feel unseen, unheard, unnoticed. They're not the first, and they're not the last. They're stuck in the middle. So that's their fear. *No one's going to see me. Nobody cares about how I feel. Nobody cares about what I think. Nobody cares about what I do.* Fours are not usually going to be the valedictorian. They're not usually interested in sports. Do you know what they're interested in? Being themselves. If you love a Four, you need to be interested in that, too, because God made them different— absolutely different. They're not always in the competitions. They just enjoy life for what it is, and that's why we need to appreciate Fours: because they remind us that it is important to be significant in life and make a difference. So their fear is going through life unnoticed and misunderstood.

How Fours Can Be Real with Self, Others, and God

So, how does a Four need to be real?

Real with Self

How do Fours need to be real with themselves? Psalm 139:14 says, "Thank you for making me so wonderfully complex! Your workmanship is marvelous—how well I know it." If you're a Four, would you do me a favor and memorize this verse and never forget it? The next time you feel sad or depressed, the next time you think you don't mean anything and you have no value, I want you to recite God's Word: *"Thank you, God, for making me so wonderfully complex. Your workmanship is marvelous."* When you call yourself worthless, you know what you're telling God? You're saying that God makes junk. God doesn't make junk, and He made you. "Your workmanship is marvelous—how well I know it."

Saul was depressed because he wasn't David. But God never created Saul to be David.

Let's just talk about Saul for a minute. Did you know Saul was an amazing dad? I know that because his son was Jonathan, and Jonathan was fantastic. Does anybody know about David's kids? They're not so good. Absalom tried to kill his dad, David.

But Jonathan was loyal to the very end—absolutely loyal. Saul raised great kids. He did great things. He did significant things. God never called him to be David. He called him to be Saul. Fours, be what God wants you to be, but don't be anybody else.

Here's the transformation you need to embrace as a Four. It's called gratitude. What is the Four focused on? What's missing. *What's wrong with me? What gifts am I missing?* So if you're a Four, you wish you were every other number because your core sin is envy. *Why can't I be a One? If I were a One, I would "should" on people so good. Why can't I be a Two? I would serve everyone. I would be like Jesus. Why can't I be a Three? I would be successful. Why can't I be a Five? A deep thinker. Why can't I be a Six? I want my core sin to be fear because at least that's reasonable. I want to be a Seven. I need to let it loose and have a good time. I want to be an Eight and tell people how I feel. I want to be a Nine and just chill.*

Why, God, did you make me a Four? Because He's God, and you're not. That's how you know when you're probably a Four, when you wish you were someone else. Pray about it, and see what God says. Then respond with gratitude. *God, thank You for making me, me. Thank You.*

Real with Others

How do Fours need to be real with others? We're raising a Four in our household, and she is our middle kid. She marches to the beat of a different drum. Your Four might not even march to a drum. It could be a harmonica. They could invent an instrument. That's what Fours do. Fours are radically different. They don't fit in your box. And that's what a lot of us do as parents. We think, *I'm going to re-create myself through my child, and they're going to have the life I always wanted.* Show me that verse. Show me the verse where God says, "Raise your child to be everything you wanted to be and have everything you wish you had." Last time I checked, all kids are God's kids. And you're a steward of the resources He's entrusted you. Fours are just different from other kids.

My daughter competed in the mountain bike state finals. We're not sure which place she took, because they all crashed at the finish line and I think the judge just guessed. It was just a pile of dust and kids. So my daughter is one of the greatest mountain bikers in the state of California. She was awesome. Afterward, she said, "Yeah, I hate it. I'm done." She's not interested in racing. Sometimes she would be racing, and she'd be in first place, and then we would lose her. What happened?

"I don't know, Dad, I was just out there, and I just started thinking."

I'm like, "You're in a race! You are in a race, and I'm a Three, and I need you to win! How on earth, in a race, do you forget where you are?"

"I don't know. I just saw a bee, and I thought I could be whatever I wanted to be."

Then one time another girl's bike broke, and my daughter stopped to help her. I was like, "What are you doing? Step on her head and go by!" Competitions don't always bring out the best in me.

My wife said, "Well, what Daddy really means is good job and way to be like Christ." Here's the thing: if you're a Four, you have to see the beauty and talent of others as a good thing.

Let me confess this to you as a sin. I'm a Three-wing-Four, so that means I want to be successful, and I'm envious of everyone else who is. That's how it works out in my life. It's great. Thanks a lot, Jesus, for making me this way. Your workmanship is marvelous, and how well I know it. I wanted to be the greatest preacher ever, and I wanted no one to be like me. And do you know what I discovered? God has a lot of amazing preachers. They're just awesome, and that irked me. That's what the sin of envy does. Envy says, "God, we need to reach out about Christ, and we will do it through me, your humble servant." But Fours, you have to see the beauty and talent of others as a good thing. All beauty reflects the glory of God, and all talent reflects the glory of God. It's okay if someone's a little better, a little more beautiful, a little more creative, a little more special than you are. It's okay because God didn't call you to be them. He called you to be you, and you reflect the glory of God just like they do but in a different way. See the beauty and the talent of others as a good thing.

There's an amazing verse that you probably never noticed in the Scriptures. It's beautiful. The conflict of the Philistines was fierce. All of Saul's days, they had battles. All his life. Take a look at 1 Samuel 14:52: "The Israelites fought constantly with the Philistines throughout Saul's lifetime. So whenever Saul observed a young man who was brave and strong, he drafted him into his army." Saul was a noticer. He saw talent, and he wasn't intimidated by it. He utilized it. That's a healthy Four. "*Oh, you're gifted. Wow! We could do amazing things for the glory of God with your gifts. Come join us.*"

One thing God had to twist in my heart was to quit seeing other people's talent as competition and instead see it as a gift. When your focus is on you, other people's talent is a threat. When your focus is on God, it's a benefit. One of the reasons I believe the church where I serve as pastor is successful is because about fifteen years ago, I had to repent from envy and say, "God, send me all the talent You can." Every single person on our executive team is an accomplished, gifted, talented leader who serves here. I've learned not to be intimidated by giftedness but to celebrate it and say, "You guys are great. Be everything God's called you to be." I don't have to know everything, do everything, and be everything. God doesn't want me to be awesome. He wants His church to be awesome. And for that to be true, we have to have an awesome team.

Just because you're a Christian doesn't mean you don't struggle with envy. Saul was the king of Israel and struggled with it deeply. You're not a king, but you can struggle.

Real with God

How do Fours need to be real with God? You have to know your place if you're a Four. You have to understand that you cannot be ruled by your emotions.

In 1 Samuel 13:8, we read this: "Saul waited there seven days for Samuel, as Samuel had instructed him earlier, but Samuel still didn't come." What happened? Samuel, who held the office of priest, told Saul to wait seven days, and then he would come and sacrifice.

Samuel promised to do it. There are only three leadership roles in the Old Testament: prophet, priest, and king. Saul was two of the three offices. He was king, and if you study his life, he was also a prophet. That's not bad. You get two of the three. Only Jesus was all three.

So here's the thing: Saul was a prophet, and he was a king. But he was not a priest. He needed to wait for the priest, Samuel, to sacrifice before he went into battle. So Saul waited there seven days for Samuel. But Samuel was a little late. Samuel had instructed him to wait, and then Samuel didn't come on time.

Have you ever prayed something like this: "Lord, I need You to answer me in the next eight minutes"? Here's what happened next: "Saul realized that his troops were rapidly slipping away. So he demanded, 'Bring me the burnt offering and the peace offerings!' And Saul sacrificed the burnt offering himself" (vv. 8–9). Saul acted as the priest. And do you know what happened? Because of his disobedience, Saul lost the role of prophet and king, and God chose David instead.

Fours, feel your emotions. God gave them to you. But follow your faith.

How Do You Love a Four?

If you have a child or a loved one who is a Four, how can you demonstrate love to that person?

1. Don't put them in a box.

It isn't going to work. I don't care how big the box is. Don't put them in a box. Allow them the freedom to be who God created them to be.

2. Enjoy and appreciate how deeply they feel.

Some of you have no hearts. You don't have any feelings. Maybe you did once. But Fours have feelings. They have emotions, right? Appreciate that, love that, and celebrate that. It's great that Fours cry in worship. Some of you are like *Star Trek*'s Mr. Spock: "Tell me how that feels." Some of you watch people in worship who raise their hands. You're like, "That's interesting." Some of you, at the height of your inspiration, when the preacher makes a profound point, you do a little golf clap and say, "Well done, Pastor, well done." If you don't know who I'm talking about, I'm talking about the Fives. But if you want to know how to love a Four, enjoy and appreciate how deeply they feel.

3. Point out how their uniqueness has blessed you.

Fours will bless your life if you let them. Tell them, "This is how you've made a difference in my life."

4. Challenge them to feel but not to be led by their feelings.

You're going to need to do this every day. "Okay, we've cried for fifty-eight minutes. That was a good cry. We've all felt the weight of your emotions. Now, I need you to do the right thing whether you feel like it or not."

5. Enjoy the ride.

It's going to be fun. Woo-hoo! Whenever I go in to talk with my daughter, who is a Four, I don't know where we're going, but I know it's going to be entertaining. The conversation usually starts with, "Nothing is wrong." And then eight hours later and lots of crying, it's awesome.

A Prayer for Fours

Here is a prayer for the Fours:

God, let me feel and experience my emotions but follow Your commands.

Look, I get it. Saul panicked; he freaked. Samuel was late. Saul should have read *The Lord of the Rings.* Wizards are never late; they arrive precisely when they need to.

Wouldn't you be freaking out if you were about to go into battle and everybody's panicking, and you're the leader, and you're waiting for Samuel, and Samuel isn't showing up? Saul was thinking, *Samuel is getting old. Did he die on the way? I can't text him. I can't call him. I don't know where he is. Maybe he forgot. I don't know.* Samuel said, *"Wait seven days, and I'll be there, and then we'll go to battle, and God will give you victory."* But Saul chose to follow his emotions, not his faith.

Fours, you need to follow your faith, not your emotions.

God, let me feel my emotions but follow Your commands. Help me see my uniqueness and love it the way You do.

Here is my prayer for you:

God, help Fours to love themselves the way You do. Help them see others' giftedness and celebrate it instead of being jealous of it. Fours are absolutely amazing, and we are blessed to have them. But if they don't get control of their emotions, they're going to throw spears at the people they love. God, the Bible says that we are to love You with all our heart, soul, mind, and strength, and we're to love our neighbor as we love ourselves. Help the Fours to love You, to love others, and to love themselves, exactly the way You made them. In Jesus' name, amen.

THE OBSERVER

Wisdom vs. Greed

I think loving ourselves is probably the hardest thing we do. We need to understand that we're not a total mess; there are actually beautiful things in our lives that reflect the glory of God. So many of us are focused on what's wrong in our lives; we're not listening to God and what He has to say about what's right. Some things are right and reflect the glory of God.

In this chapter, we are going to talk about Fives, the Observers, who live in their minds. Coming to the Five is the biggest shift in the Enneagram so far. If you're a Four and you're married to a Five and you feel separate from them at times, there's a reason for that. It is because there's a gigantic gap. Don't be discouraged, because often Fours and Fives fall in love. Why? Opposites attract. And then you drive yourself crazy for the rest of your lives. But there's something about that. The Four feels more deeply than any other type in the heart triad. So as we shift to the Five, we see people who do not live their lives based on their hearts, but their heads.

The Five, the Six, and the Seven live in their minds. They think about the world, and they process everything in their heads. Just know that if you're a Four, and you're married to a Five, you're going to be talking about how you feel, and the Five is going to be talking about what they think. That often creates a gap that feels insurmountable, but don't believe that because it's vitally important.

Fives in the Bible: Nicodemus

Even if you've never been to a church, you've probably seen the Bible verse John 3:16 at a football game, basketball game, or baseball game: "For this is how God loved the world: He gave his one and only Son, so that everyone who believes in him will not perish but have eternal life." This amazing verse is part of a conversation that takes place one night between Nicodemus, a brilliant man, and the only person who can save mankind, Jesus Christ.

I believe that Nicodemus is a Five, an Observer. For the last three chapters, we've been in the heart section of the Enneagram: the Twos, the Threes, and the Fours. Their underlying issue is, "How do I feel?" For the Two, it's based on serving. For the Three, it's based on achieving. For the Four, it's just about feeling. *Do I feel like I'm making a difference? Do I feel like I have depth? Do I feel creative?*

Jesus Christ is going to try to get Nicodemus out of his head and into his heart. And that's where the idea "born again" comes from. Nicodemus learns that he cannot think his way into heaven. He would never experience the life that God had for him unless he was born again.

If you're a Five, God has given you a beautiful mind. You're an Observer, you're a deep thinker, and you are loved and appreciated, but you have to get in contact with your heart. Because despite what you think, if you're a Five, you do have emotions and feelings. How do I know that? Because Fives who are scientists tell us no human being ever makes a decision without emotion. Though it's difficult to observe emotions in the Fives, they're there. You just can't see them clearly. Trust me, Fives, you're not Mr. Spock. You have a heart, and you need to get in touch with it.

The story of Nicodemus begins like this: "There was a man named Nicodemus, a Jewish religious leader who was a Pharisee" (John 3:1). Now, this sentence really doesn't help us out. In the Greek, it's more like a list of accomplishments. For example, if Nicodemus were a guest speaker at a college, his bio would specify him as a PhD along with a long list of accomplishments and awards. Nicodemus was world renowned for his intelligence. He was brilliant, a mind above almost every other mind. He was a Jewish religious leader. But not just *a* leader—he was one of *the* leading Pharisees. In fact, Nicodemus was even part of the Sanhedrin. Why is that important, you might ask? Imagine an American citizen who's a member of the US Senate and the Supreme Court at the same time. I don't even know if that's constitutionally possible, so don't send me an email. I'm just saying it would be like that. So as someone akin to a senator and Supreme Court justice, Nicodemus is a very powerful person, and he is brilliant.

Verse 2 says, "After dark one evening, he came to speak with Jesus." I want you to notice that phrase, "dark one evening," because when you read the gospel of John, *light* never means the literal lights are on, and *dark* never means the lights are off. John was speaking metaphorically, pointing out how during one of the darkest times in history, one of the greatest minds of the Jews is missing out on who Jesus is. If you're a Five, you cannot think your way into heaven, and many of you will miss heaven by eighteen inches—that's roughly the distance from your brain to your heart. Now I'm sure some of the Fives are going to start calculating, *Well, my height is actually 5 feet, 11 inches* . . . Okay, okay, smart guy. I don't know the exact distance between your brain and your heart, but you get it: I need you to connect with your heart.

When Nicodemus, one of the most educated individuals and accomplished leaders in Israel's history, came to speak with Jesus, he addressed Him as Rabbi. He acknowledged Jesus' brilliance. "'Rabbi,' he said, 'we all know that God has sent you to teach us. Your miraculous signs are evidence that God is with you'" (John 3:2).

What do the Fives do? Fives watch the world we live in. They make observations, and they take note of them. Nicodemus said, "Your miraculous signs are evidence that God is with you." It doesn't take a genius to see someone raise someone from the dead and say, "Well, you're kind of special." If I raised somebody from the dead, I hope people would say, "You know that Matt Brown? He's special." Nicodemus said, "Your miraculous signs are evidence that God is with you," to which Jesus replied, "I tell you the truth, unless you are born again, you cannot see the Kingdom of God" (3:3).

There Nicodemus was, making observations. He was looking at the world as he understood it, and Jesus told him you can't observe your way into heaven. This is why so many intellectuals don't come to faith in Christ. You can be a professor of the New Testament and teach students about Christianity and still miss Jesus.

During my first semester in college, I took a New Testament class. I'll never forget when the professor wrote on the board: "Satan is not real." And I thought, *What? That's crazy.* Then I looked around and saw that everybody in the class was taking notes. I said, "Why are you guys taking notes? This guy's nuts." My professor could tell based on my face and my inability to hide my Three, and he asked, "You have a different opinion?" I said, "No, but Jesus did. So I'm going to go with Jesus." As you can imagine, I didn't do too well in that class, but I got through it.

A lot of intellectuals know a lot about the Bible, and they know nothing about God. Because you can't wrap your mind around God, your brain ain't big enough. I did just write "ain't," and if you are a Five—that's going to kill you.

Jesus said, "Unless you are born again, you cannot see the Kingdom of God" (v. 3). Something has to happen dramatically in you, and there has to be a real change for you to get into heaven. You can't think your way in, you can't earn your way in, and you can't buy your way in.

Nicodemus said what a Five would say: "'What do you mean?' exclaimed Nicodemus. 'How can an old man go back into his mother's womb and be born again?'" (v. 4). He knew that was impossible. He wouldn't fit.

"Jesus replied, 'I assure you, no one can enter the Kingdom of God without being born of water and the Spirit'" (v. 5). What was Jesus talking about?

Think about this: What happens right before you're born? Have you ever experienced that? I can tell you because I was there for my first child's birth. Tammy felt birth pain. She told me it was time to go to the hospital. We panicked and rushed to the hospital. The doctors checked her out, and they said, "No baby today; she's not cooked yet. You need to go home."

We were frustrated, and Tammy was hungry, so we went to a restaurant called Coco's. Tammy stood up to go to the bathroom and said, "Oh no, it happened." Her water broke. And let me just tell you this, young men: it's not a small amount of water. I had to add a few dollars to our tip and apologize profusely to the management and all the other people eating dinner as my wife leaked across the carpet as we tried to get out of the restaurant. And she didn't stop leaking. We got into a van, and she was like a hose.

So when you're born, the water breaks. You are born of water, and then guess what happens? You come out into the world.

Unless the Spirit is involved in your conversion, you haven't been born again. It doesn't matter if you walk forward at an evangelistic crusade or get baptized at your church; without the Spirit, you just took a walk or you just got wet, but you are not saved. Something has to happen with the Spirit. There's an interaction between you and God where new life begins. Jesus said, "Humans can reproduce only human life, but the Spirit gives birth to spiritual life" (v. 6).

There's only one person who can get you to God. For the past twenty years, I've driven past a building with "Palm Readers" on the sign out front. Recently I noticed that sign had been changed to "Spiritual Guide." Be very careful about who you choose for a spiritual guide because if you choose the wrong one, that person will not lead you to heaven but straight to hell. Don't believe someone just because they claim to be spiritually wise.

Nicodemus was supposed to be a spiritual guide for Israel. He was the best they had. He was the smartest, and he could write Hebrew forward and backward. He knew Greek, and he could speak Aramaic. He was brilliant beyond brilliant—and he was completely missing it.

Jesus said, "The Holy Spirit gives birth to spiritual life. So don't be surprised when I say, 'You must be born again.' The wind blows wherever it wants. Just as you can hear the wind but can't tell where it comes from or where it is going, so you can't explain how people are born of the Spirit" (vv. 6–8). If you're a Five and Observer, you can't explain how people are born of the Spirit. What does that mean?

It's sad that, as Christians, we argue over how people are saved. Jesus just said we are never going to understand it fully. I don't care what the commentary says. There is some interaction between God and us that produces life. Churches fight over what is God's part and what is our part, and we miss out on the experience of the Spirit.

"'How are these things possible?' Nicodemus asked" (v. 9). What was Nicodemus doing? He was still observing. He was detached, and he was watching.

"Jesus replied, 'You are a respected Jewish teacher, and yet you don't understand these things?'" (v. 10). If you're a college student, there are some things your professors . . . wait for it . . . don't know. It's true. They don't know everything, even if they're considered some of the greatest intellectual minds in academia. In Nicodemus, we have Israel's genius, who was clueless as to what Jesus was talking about.

Jesus said, "I assure you, we tell you what we know and have seen, and yet you won't believe our testimony. But if you don't believe me when I tell you about earthly things, how can you possibly believe if I tell you about heavenly things? No one has ever gone to heaven and returned. But the Son of Man has come down from heaven" (vv. 11–13). Why is Jesus a reliable guide? Because He's taking you to where He is from. Everybody else is just guessing. But Jesus is reliable.

Jesus continued, "As Moses lifted up the bronze snake on a pole in the wilderness, so the Son of Man must be lifted up, so that everyone who believes in him will have eternal life" (vv. 14–15).

And then we get to that familiar verse: "For this is how God loved the world: He gave his one and only Son, so that everyone who believes in him will not perish but have eternal life" (v. 16). That's the gospel.

How do you get to heaven from here? It's a heart issue. You can't think your way in.

The Character of Fives: They Reflect God's Wisdom

Fives are amazing and incredible. Often they are geniuses. Fives reflect God's wisdom. The reality is they're probably smarter than the rest of us.

The Core Motivation of Fives: Knowledge

What drives Fives? What is their core motivation? They want to gain knowledge.

Why was Nicodemus talking to Jesus? Because he couldn't wrap his mind around Jesus, and who can? Who can take lunch from a little boy and feed five thousand people? Who does that? Jesus. It doesn't make any sense. Who walks on water? Try it. One of my favorite things is to watch people on Instagram trying to do it. No one does it. They all fall into the water, every time. It's hilarious.

Fives are trying to gain knowledge. They're trying to understand. If you're raising a little Five, guess what their favorite question is going to be: "Why?" You're like, "Wow, he's four years old and smarter than all of us." You're raising a little Einstein. Just get out of the way and watch him or her go.

Fives want to know why the world is like it is. Others don't care. I don't need to know how a plane works; I just want it to work. But Fives make great pilots. You want a Five at the wheel when that thing isn't working.

Fives want to know why. They ask big questions. "Why are things this way?" And it's that question that led to seminaries, which led to universities, which led to science. It's sad that in these modern days we give Christianity no credit, but the reality is it was great Christians who asked great questions that led to our great schools that transformed human life. Fives want to know why things work the way they do.

Fives want to uncover the truth. Don't ever take a Five to a magic show. The Five will say, "Oh, I know exactly how they did it." And the rest of us are like, "Shut up! We want to believe." But Fives want to uncover the truth. They are great detectives. "How did this happen? How do I figure out who committed the crime?"

When Fives are healthy, they're insightful and observant, desiring for the world to be less chaotic and more organized.

Here's the shift when Fives become unhealthy—and just so you know, we're all unhealthy. Unhealthy Fives shift from being observant to detached. So if you're raising a kid who is a Five, you really have to watch video games because your child will disappear into books and computers to think. Those things make sense; people don't. People are erratic, weird, and bizarre, so Fives tend to retreat deeper into themselves. You've got to make sure that you love them and care for them, but you call them out and say, "We need you to be with us, even if it's for five minutes." Fives want to eat their meals in their room, and they don't understand why you guys want to interact while you eat. It's inefficient, and you can't read while you do that.

Unhealthy Fives do not engage emotionally or socially in

healthy ways. When you're a healthy Five, you'll go to the party and stand in the corner and watch everyone. But when you become unhealthy, you're not going to the party. You're not going anywhere, and you retreat into yourself.

Fives Need to Be Competent

Fives need to be competent. Why was Nicodemus there? Because he didn't get it. *"Jesus, I don't understand why I don't see what everyone else is seeing. Can You explain that to me?"* They need to avoid incompetence because it can cause them to withdraw completely from the world around them.

Have you noticed people are incompetent? One of my favorite conversations ever was at a fast-food restaurant where I was trying to order a medium milkshake. The server said, "What would you like, sir?"

I said, "I would like a medium milkshake."

She said, "I'm sorry, sir. We only have one size."

I said, "What size cup would that one-size milkshake come in?"

She said, "It would be a medium, sir."

That's a true story.

Fives Focus on Decisions and Processing

When Fives are healthy, they remain calm and focused on decisions and processing. That's why you want a Five flying the plane when both engines have gone bad. You don't want me. I'm screaming, "We're gonna die! We're gonna die!" The Five calmly calls the tower and says, "We lost engine one. We lost engine two. Tower, we're going to need an emergency landing. We're descending at a speed of three thousand feet per second. I'm going to need you to have an ambulance and fire engines ready as we land." Right? Have you ever listened to Captain Sully? He calmly landed that plane in the Hudson River and saved everyone on board because he didn't panic, and he knew what to do. He calmly said, "We're gonna be in the Hudson."[1]

You want your emergency room doctors to be Fives. "Okay, sir, you've lost a left leg and a right arm, and one ear." A doctor who is a Four says, "Oh my gosh, you must be hurting so bad. I am so sorry." A Three says, "You're going to die. I'm not operating. This guy's as good as dead. This is not going on my record." A One says, "You know, you shouldn't have done that. That's why we wear helmets."

The Five remains calm and focused and can remain unemotional. When your small group is ready to kill each other, the Fives are like, "I think we have a problem." Fours are choking each other out. Threes are looking for an open group.

If you're married to a Five, here's why you fell in love with them: they're very thoughtful. They think a lot, so they have knowledge in multiple areas, which makes them incredibly perceptive. If you're a Four and you're married to a Five, the reason you fell in love with them is they can observe your uniqueness and they like it. You're different, and they love that about you. It's beautiful. They can listen. Well, they can repeat back to you how you feel, what you're thinking, and what's happening in your life.

The Core Sin of Fives: Greed

If you're a Five, you're not going to like your core sin. I mean, who likes theirs? The core sin of the Five is greed. What do I mean by that? Fives tend to be stingy. Often, what the Five does is withhold. They withhold first and foremost their time. So don't waste it.

If you're a dad or a mom and you're a Five, you don't have time for the kids. You're busy providing for their lives. And you need time to study, time to grow, time to learn, and you retreat to yourself. You don't share time. You're greedy with your time. If you're a Five, you're going to have difficulty serving at the church. It is going to be hard for you to volunteer because you will be surrounded by incompetence.

If you love someone who is a Five, they're going to be greedy or stingy with their emotions—they hold them in. They do have a heart, but sharing their feelings is scary, and often if you love this person it's like loving them while they're on the other side of the glass. They let you in slowly. So if you're a Five, you have to learn to be generous with your time and generous with your emotions. Fives, if someone says "I love you" to you, you can't respond, "Well, I said it once eight years ago. That should be sufficient." No, that is not sufficient.

Fives are greedy with their knowledge. Fives have a hard time sharing what they know because it's precious to them; it's something they've learned; it's something they've attained. And let me tell you something: if you are a Five, you make a great teacher, a great professor, because you can make us all better. You can share what you know, you can share what you've learned, especially if you're a Christian. You can teach people about God because you understand how it works because you've studied it. If you're a Five, what good is studying the Bible from front to back if you never share it with anyone? It's not just for you; it's meant to be shared.

Fives can also be greedy with their money. Fives hold it. Often, Fives are great savers because they're stingy. They calculate the tithe and the tip. They have a hard time being generous and just blessing somebody with something. Fives have to learn to be generous. A healthy Five is in pursuit of generosity and growth. But growth doesn't stop till you die. When God's done with you—the day you die, and you're in heaven—you can stop growing. God's going to transform you. God's going to change you. God's going to complete you. But until that time, you have to keep growing. A healthy Five is always in pursuit of generosity.

We don't know much about Nicodemus; he's only mentioned a couple of times in the Bible. The first time is John 3, where he had a conversation with Jesus in the middle of the night, and he was trying to understand Jesus. The second time is in John 7, when the Jewish leaders were trying to kill Jesus. Nicodemus observed that Jesus was not getting a fair trial, and he spoke up for Jesus.

We don't know if he became a believer, but we know that when Jesus was crucified, and His body was taken off the cross, the tomb was provided by a man named Joseph of Arimathea, and the funeral expenses were paid for by Nicodemus. John 19:39 says, "With him came Nicodemus, the man who had come to Jesus at night. He brought about seventy-five pounds of perfumed ointment made from myrrh and aloes." I tried to figure out how to calculate the value of the oils that Nicodemus brought. Scholars argue that it could be anywhere between fifty thousand American dollars and a half a million dollars that Nicodemus spent burying Jesus. Why? I believe, eventually, Jesus got from Nicodemus's head to his heart, and he was transformed. So he was generous with Jesus. He was generous with his money. He paid for it.

Nicodemus also became generous with his time. On the eve of Passover, where was Nicodemus? He was burying Jesus, expressing grief with Joseph of Arimathea. With his knowledge, Nicodemus knew what to do. He knew—wait for it—how a king should be buried. Jesus was buried as a king, with seventy-five pounds of rare oil, which makes the resurrection all the more amazing.

Fives Avoid Incompetence

What does a Five want to avoid? At all costs, they must avoid incompetence.

You want to throw off a Five? Yell, "Pop quiz!" They're going to pop you. They want to be ready. They want to be prepared. They want to know when the test is and when the papers are due. And you had better stick to the syllabus. They want to avoid incompetence.

Fives Fear Being Embarrassed

Don't ever embarrass a Five. They don't like it. The reason Nicodemus came at night must have been because he was not interested in the religious and political theatrics of the day. Nicodemus knew Jesus was smart and had seen his contemporaries get embarrassed by Jesus as they questioned Him during the day. Nicodemus had questions and knew Jesus had answers. But the conversation had to be on his terms. How amazing it is that He was willing to meet Nicodemus on his terms. Why? Because He loves Fives! Thank God we have a Savior who is willing to meet us where we are! If you want your Fives to come out of their shells, don't embarrass them. They will retreat further and further from social interaction. And here's the thing: Since Fives know almost everything, guess what the rest of us are trying to do? Find when they're wrong so we can point and say, "You don't know everything." They're not coming over to game night at your house. They didn't want to come in the first place. Notice that even when Jesus challenges what Nicodemus is ignorant of, He still refers to him as teacher. Jesus wasn't interested in wining an argument or proving a point. He wanted to save a soul.

How Fives Can Be Real with
Self, Others, and God

How do you need to be real with yourself, others, and God if you're a Five?

Real with Self

Fives need to get out of their heads and in touch with their emotions. If you are raising a child who is a Five, remember that Fives don't act out—they act in. The unhealthier they get, the more they will retreat into themselves. Fives must pursue people and relationships. Relationships with a Five can be incredible, but help them unpack their emotions.

If you love a Five, say to them, "I hear what you're saying. Tell me, how does that make you feel?" The Five will give you the facts. *Here's the budget. Here's when we're going. Here's our retirement plan. Here's my job. Here are the pros and the cons. Here's what it says on Wikipedia.*

That's great. How does that make you feel?

Invite them to talk about how they feel, and make it a safe place. Fives need to get out of their heads and in touch with their emotions.

The problem is, facts feel safe and are reliable; feelings are erratic and often feel embarrassing. Encourage them to explore how they feel and study their emotions. Invite them out of their heads.

Real with Others

Here's how Fives need to be real with others. I encourage you to memorize this verse, and if you're a Five, I'm sure you will: "One who separates himself seeks his own desire; he quarrels against all sound wisdom" (Proverbs 18:1 NASB). Nowhere in the Bible does God call you to live for yourself. He calls you to die to yourself.

When you're on your own, you get dumber, not smarter. There is no correlation in sociology between IQ and morality. Do you know what they found? People are not better people when they're smarter. They're just better at convincing themselves that what they're doing isn't wrong. So if you got a smart kid, it doesn't mean that kid is going to be good; it just means it's going to be hard to catch that kid doing wrong because he or she is smart.

What does this mean if you're a Five? You don't want to be in a small group because there are dumb people in there. But they understand life in many ways better than you do, and they can draw out things that you'll miss, because you will never be who God called you to be by yourself with your Bible in your backyard.

You cannot worship a God who *is* community if you're on your own. The prayer of Jesus is not that you would be one with Him by yourself. The prayer of Jesus is that "they will all be one, just as you and I are one—as you are in me, Father, and I am in you" (John 17:21). That's the prayer. Fives, you've got to press into community and press into relationships. You've got to make yourself available for date night, for talking, for relationships, for conversation. Even if it's exhausting, and even if you think everyone is incompetent, press in. Even Jesus was occasionally impressed with people.

Real with God

In 2 Timothy 3:7, Paul described people who are "always learning and never able to come to the knowledge of the truth" (NASB). Fives, you can know everything there is in the Bible, and you still might know nothing about God.

And how do we know that? Because Jesus stood before Pharisees and said, "You search the Scriptures because you think they give you eternal life. But the Scriptures point to me! Yet you refuse to come to me to receive this life" (John 5:39–40). You need to learn.

If you're a Five, connect with God in worship. I get it; it's scary. The songs are kind of mushy. Worship can feel a little emotional. It will be fine; embrace it. Connect with God with your heart. Connect with God through your emotions. Not every song and not every sermon needs to be dissected. Sometimes you just need to feel what God has to say. Sometimes you just need to experience where the Spirit is moving. Remember, Jesus said to Nicodemus that the wind blows where it wishes. For Fives, you don't always need to analyze the Spirit's movement; sometimes you just need to feel God's wind on your face.

How Do You Love a Five?

So how do you love a Five?

1. Acknowledge their need for personal space and time.

This is probably the most important thing you have to acknowledge: Fives need personal space and time. It's not that they hate you. It's just that they love time with themselves.

I have a friend who is a Five. He has a deal with his wife that he gets in his Jeep and drives out to the desert by himself. I could do that for about forty-five seconds. I would go insane. I'm not going to the desert by myself. Fives who are reading this probably think, *That sounds great. I've never thought of that. I'll get a Jeep. I'm going to get a Jeep this week.*

I have another friend who gets two weeks of vacation every year. One week he spends with his kids, and one week a year he spends by himself. My wife would kill me.

If you have a kid who is a Five, that kid is going to need his or her own time, especially if your kids share a room. You have to give Fives their own time and their own space.

2. Express how much it means to you when they engage.

Don't say, "Well, it's about time. Oh, look at who's finally here. Smarty-pants decided to join us for fun and family night." If you do that, you've embarrassed them. You just shamed them, and guess what they're going to do? They're not coming back. Encourage them when they do engage. Tell them how much it means. Say, "Thank you so much for joining us. It means so much when you come. I know groups exhaust you. I know parties wear you out. It means so much that you're here. Thank you."

3. Don't invite them to big parties.

And if you're married to a Five, don't throw big parties. Have parties with smaller groups because Fives come alive in a smaller group. If you have a thousand people, the Fives will be over in the corner just waiting for it to be over. Remember that Fives like information and observation, and a big party has neither of those things. It's okay for you to love to celebrate and cut loose in your way, but learn to celebrate and cut loose with a Five.

My good friend Tom is a Five. We love each other, but we are very different. When he bought a new car, he sat in the car and read the entire owner's manual from front to back. Let me tell you, any car you will ever purchase from me, I cannot guarantee the condition of the car, but I can guarantee the condition of the owner's manual—it has never been opened. It is in precisely the same spot from the moment I bought the car because when I buy a new car, I want to drive it. But Tom said, "I love sitting in my new car and reading every page of the manual. It has all this amazing information." There are things in my car that I will never know what they do. I have at least eighteen buttons in my car that I don't know what they do. I tell my kids, "Don't press that button; we might die." But my friend Tom comes alive when there are new buttons to press. So when I hang with Tom, he wants to show me everything his new car can do, and he knows everything it can do!

4. Don't criticize the way they have fun.

If you're going on a vacation, a Five may want to know every single thing about every town: the history of that town, who died, who got killed, who got married there, what happened. You're saying, "I just wanted to go to the pier." But Fives are going to geek out on that stuff. They'll say, "Oh my gosh, this post is a thousand years old. It was first constructed by . . ." And you thought it was just a pier.

5. Utilize their knowledge and wisdom.

If you're dumb, the greatest gift you could give to yourself is to become friends with a Five. Fives are awesome and usually brilliant! And if you're like me and you talk a lot, they're great friends because they have room for the air that comes out of your mouth. Do you know what exhausts me? Someone like me. I need a Five because I like to talk, and they let me. The problem is not getting me to open up and tell you what I know; the challenge is getting a Five to open up and tell what they know, and if you want a Five to talk, you have to be very specific and leave space for them to speak.

A Prayer for Fives

I want to challenge you, Fives, to pray this week:

God, help me connect my heart to Yours. Help me feel more deeply and embrace the mystery of who You are.

You're never going to be able to fully understand God. So pray,

Help me to have grace for people who are incompetent, and change my heart on community group night.

We need you, Fives. God has given you a beautiful mind, but you have to share it with us; otherwise, we don't get to be blessed by it. Here's my prayer for you.

Holy Father, thank You for the awesome, incredible gift of the Fives. We're so thankful for the way they see the world. We're thankful for the way they operate and the way they can help us connect with You intellectually. Fives can draw out of us thoughts that we never knew we had. So, Lord, help us encourage Fives to join with us in community and to participate in the chaos of relationship. We pray this in Jesus' name, amen.

THE LOYALIST

Faithfulness vs. Fear

You are not an accident.

There are no such thing as accidental children—just accidental parents. God made you. He knows you and loves you. God loves you because you are gifted and beautiful, and God loves you despite your brokenness. God pursues you, and He'll never stop pursuing you, because He cares about you and He's designed you to be with Him forever.

If fear is a part of your life, if it's something that's influencing your life maybe even more than your faith, know that God doesn't want you to be led by fear. He wants you to be led by Him.

Many of us are afraid to step out in faith. We're afraid to take a risk, and we're afraid to step into the realm of what's unseen. So let's look at the Six.

Sixes in the Bible: Peter

In this chapter, we are going to take a look at the life of the apostle Peter. Peter is one of the most amazing people ever to live. He's a Loyalist, a Six on the Enneagram. He was somebody who wanted so desperately to be there, to be stable, but he was riddled with fear, even when knowing the power and promise he witnessed in Jesus constantly.

In our world today, we have a crisis of obesity. It doesn't matter what country you are in; obesity is one of the great ills that the world is facing. Two thousand years ago, obesity was not an issue— starvation was. It didn't matter whether you lived in Europe, India, or Africa, starving to death was a possibility for everyone, whether you were rich or poor, powerful or a slave.

And so, in Matthew 14, Jesus did something amazing. People were hungry, some of them were starving. He took a couple of fish and a few loaves of bread, blessed them, and fed the masses. They freaked out. All their problems were solved! They wanted to take Jesus and make Him king. So immediately, Jesus did something surprising.

Matthew 14:22 says, "Immediately after this, Jesus insisted that his disciples get back into the boat and cross to the other side of the lake, while he sent the people home." If power is something that you aspire to, if fame is important to you, I want you to know that Jesus always ran from both. He ran from fame, and He ran from power, because those things can corrupt even the greatest of intentions. You can have a pure heart when you start out young—a heart to serve, to give, to take care of people. And then you get elected, you get a position, you get power, and your motives change. Jesus told the disciples, *"Let's get out of here. I know you're wowed by what I just did, but we have to head across the lake."*

Jesus sent the people home, because the party's over when Jesus says it's over. "After sending them home, he went up into the hills by himself to pray. Night fell while he was there alone" (v. 23). Jesus got alone with God, and He prayed until nightfall. Meanwhile, the disciples were in trouble far away from land. Where were they? They were on the Sea of Galilee.

If you go to Israel, you might be a little disappointed when you see the Sea of Galilee.

The Eskimos have five hundred words for snow because snow is around them all the time. If you live in Alaska, there is a lot of snow. If you live in the Middle East, there is not a lot of water, so you don't need a lot of words for water. The Jews call everything a "sea," whether it's a lake, an ocean, or the Mediterranean. The Sea of Galilee is just a lake. So when you go there after you have read the story, you might think, *How the heck do you almost die in the Sea of Galilee? Just swim to the shore. It's not that big a deal.*

Well, here's what happened. "The disciples were in trouble far away from land, for a strong wind had risen, and they were fighting heavy waves" (v. 24). Let me tell you; it doesn't take much of a wave to scare you to death. Waves can be very terrifying. When I took my kids surfing when they were little, my daughter yelled, "Dad, I'm gonna die!" It was like a one-foot wave. But moving water is stronger than you, it's more powerful than you, and it can terrify you.

About fifteen years ago, Tammy and I got certified for diving. It was going to be great—a new adventure. We went through all the classes. And to get certified in diving, you pretty much just learn all the ways that you can kill yourself while diving. You need to know the math. You need to know what's going on so you don't put yourself or others in danger out in the ocean. God made us to remain above water, not below it. When you go below the water, bad things can happen.

Tammy and I passed certification, and it was a blast. We had a good time learning, and we went for our first dive without an instructor. That meant Tammy and I were our own experts. We were supposed to save ourselves; that's what it meant. We went to Catalina Island off the coast of California. It wasn't super adventurous or super dangerous. It's like five feet from Long Beach, so it wasn't scary, right?

We were having a wonderful dive and a really great time. We were down below in the ocean, looking at all kinds of fish and sea life. What we didn't know was that a storm was brewing above. We had no idea that a summer storm came in, and it was blowing our boat all over the place. So we surfaced, and we were surprised by this storm that had whipped up instantaneously. The ocean went from flat to four-foot waves.

Now, that doesn't sound terrifying when you read about it, but when you're in the ocean, and your head is twelve inches above the water, as you bob, every four-foot wave is, guess what? Four feet over your head. Every wave that comes over you kind of drowns you and pushes you down.

By this time, we were all out of oxygen. My wife, who's a Six, assessed the situation and said, "We are going to die!" Now, Tammy is an influential person and the cofounder of our church; people look up to her. When she announces that we're all doomed, that's bad news. She screamed, "I'm going to die, we're going to die, and our children are going to be raised without parents!"

I tried to talk her off this mountain of fear. There was another couple with us, and they were just treading water, watching us. The other couple's husband panicked, and he swam off and left his wife. His actions were like, "Honey, you're on your own." He started swimming toward the boat. And there I was with two women. One was flipping out. The other one was just looking at me.

I said to her, "Where's your husband?"

She's said, "He's gone."

I said, "Okay, just hang with me."

I flipped Tammy upside down on her back, and I started swimming, dragging her while she's crying, "I'm going to die! I'm going to die! You did this!" We were swimming, swimming, swimming, swimming, swimming, and finally, just when we couldn't do it any longer, someone on the boat threw us a lifeline. I grabbed onto the lifeline and pulled us into the boat. Our friend got up on the boat, and there was her husband, standing there. He helped his wife up to the boat, and she smacked him right in the nose. "Don't you ever leave me again!" It was great.

Tammy said, "We will never do that again." And because she's a powerful person, we have not gone diving again.

So let me just say that waves can be scary. It doesn't take a gigantic hurricane to die, okay? Some of you can drown in a swimming pool if someone does a cannonball. Water is scary. A lot of people die crossing a river because they think, *Oh, the water is only waist deep.* Well, when you're standing up, it's waist deep. When you're lying flat, you're in big trouble.

So just know it can get very scary, very quickly.

Let's look back at our story in the Bible. In Matthew 14:24, "A strong wind had risen, and they were fighting heavy waves." Jesus fed the five thousand probably about dinnertime, because He likely preached when the sun was out. The people ate as the sun was going down. So this storm had been going on for hours, and the disciples were exhausted. They were terrified, they didn't know what to do, and they were going to drown.

Look what happened next: "About three o'clock in the morning Jesus came toward them, walking on the water" (v. 25). Some people say, "This is scientifically impossible, and this is one of the reasons I don't believe the Bible." Okay, listen to me, Captain Smarty-Pants. The most challenging verse in the Bible is the very first verse—Genesis 1:1: "In the beginning God created the heavens and the earth." If you can get past that, everything else is easy. Because if God can create water, I think He can walk on it. He can do whatever He wants with it.

Jesus was walking toward the disciples on the water, which was a little freaky. It was three o'clock in the morning. The disciples thought they were going to die, and now here came Jesus, walking on water. When the disciples saw Him, they were terrified, as you would be—as we all would be. We would all be scared to death if we think we're going to die, and here comes somebody walking on the water. This doesn't happen.

Can you imagine that you go out to a local lake for an afternoon barbecue, and all of a sudden you see me out there walking on water? You'd be like, *Wow.*

How did the disciples respond? "When the disciples saw him walking on the water, they were terrified. In their fear, they cried out, 'It's a ghost!'" (v. 26). Notice the phrase "In their fear." This is where some of you live every single day. You live in your fear. In your marriage, you're in fear. Raising your kids, you're in fear. As a college student, you're in fear. In your friendships, you're in fear. When you're on the Internet, you're attracted to fear.

This is why our news is the way it is. Every night, the news at eleven reports that you're going to die, right? Every single night you're going to die. People are freaked out.

So in the disciples' fear, they cried out, "It's a ghost!" The next verse says, "But Jesus spoke to them at once. 'Don't be afraid,' he said. 'Take courage. I am here!'" (v. 27). Over 360 times in the Bible, God says the words, "Don't be afraid." That's almost one time for every day of the year.

Don't be afraid, don't be afraid, don't be afraid. Why would God keep saying that? Because you're freaking out. God says, "Don't be afraid. Take courage." A lot of us think courage is something we either have or we don't have. We look at courage the way we look at happiness. Both courage and happiness take work. You have to work toward them.

Jesus said, "Don't be afraid. Take courage." Why? These are some of the most important words for every single one of us who believes in God: "I am here!"

One of the most ridiculous things we do in a church service is a thing called the invocation. It's where we invite God to be a part of what we're doing. We don't have to invite God to be with us. He's already here. You don't have to worry; He's here.

If you're a believer, you don't have to ask God to join you in your marriage; He's there. You don't have to ask God to join you in raising your children; He's there. You don't have to ask God to be with you in your finances; He's there. What you need to do is remember that He's there and act accordingly.

"Then Peter called to him, 'Lord, if it's really you . . .'" (v. 28). I mean, who else is it going to be? Think about it: if you're at a lake and you see someone walking on the water, I'm hoping you guess it's Jesus. There's a historical precedent, right?

Yes, Jesus was walking on water; this is what He does. Peter said, "Lord, if it's really you, tell me to come to you, walking on the water" (v. 28). Now, let me just say this. Be careful what you pray about. When you're flying on an airplane, don't ask God to increase your faith. And certainly don't do it when we are flying together. That is not when I want our faith to increase. I want to have very little faith as we're flying. When we land, then you can pray that all you want.

Peter said, "Lord, if it's really you, tell me to come to you." Here's the thing you need to know: God never called you to live an ordinary life. He has made every single one of you extraordinary. And He has called every single one of you to be extraordinary. So if you ask God to save you from your ordinary life and to do extraordinary things with you, guess what He's going to do? He's going to answer that request. He's going to say, "Did You hear that, Jesus? Did You hear that prayer? They want Me to do something extraordinary. Let's do it."

Peter was saying, *"Jesus, I want to walk on water like You're doing. I want to do what You do."* And just so you know, this is what Jesus made you to do. He made you to do the same things He does. And Jesus said to Peter, "Yes, come" (v. 29).

"So Peter went over the side of the boat and walked on the water toward Jesus" (v. 29). Peter went over the side of the boat. It wasn't beautiful, but he got out of the boat, and he walked on water. I'm sure he cried out, "I'm walking!" Right? Too bad it's not on Instagram because I would post this for everyone to see.

Peter started walking on water. He was doing great; it was amazing. "But when he saw the strong wind and the waves, he was terrified and began to sink" (v. 30). When Peter was focused on Jesus, he had faith. When he looked at the things that were happening, he was scared to death. And this is how things happen in every single one of our lives.

It's easy to have faith in your marriage when you're focused on Jesus. When you're looking at who you married—*Oh, we're sinking.*

It's easy to have faith in your finances when you're focused on Jesus, but when you look at your bank account—*Oh, we're bankrupt.*

It's easy to have faith, students, when you're sitting in church. It's another thing when you're actually on your campus.

Where is your faith, really? Faith is always faith when there's wind and waves. It's not faith when the sea is calm. It's faith when things are difficult. It's faith when things are scary. It's faith when the doctor says, "We need to talk about your test." That's when faith comes.

"When [Peter] saw the strong wind and the waves, he was terrified and began to sink. 'Save me, Lord!' he shouted" (v. 30). Aren't you glad Jesus isn't an unhealthy One, saying, "Well, you shouldn't have gotten out of the boat"?

"Jesus immediately reached out and grabbed him" (v. 31). I love this—"mmediately." Because Jesus is our Savior, He saves us every day. Some of you don't even know what He saved you from today.

Now, Peter was sinking. It wasn't the time for a lesson, right? When somebody's drowning, that's not the time to rehash all the events that have led to this. When your kid's in the pool going under, you don't say, "Hey, this is why we talked about this." Anybody raising little kids? You put floaties on little kids; they think they can swim. Parents, have you ever had a kid who eats lunch and then forgets to put the floaties back on?

When your kid is going under the water, that's not the time to be like, "Sweetie, this is why . . ." Because what are they going to hear? Instead you dive in *immediately* because you're a good parent. You care about your kids, so that's when you go in.

I remember when my kids were little, we had a birthday swim

party. Parents, in case you didn't know, kids lie. I asked all the kids, "Can you swim?" Every kid said, "Yep." So I was like, "Okay, everybody in the pool."

I was cooking hot dogs when I heard a sound. *Gurgle, gurgle.* I looked in the middle of the pool, and one of the biggest kids was down at the bottom.

I asked, "What is he doing? Olympics? Is he doing the underground swim thing?"

Tammy looked and said, "He's drowning!"

I said, "No, no. He told me he could swim. He's just playing games."

She said, "Get in there and save him!"

And we did. We pulled him out, and he threw up.

I said, "You said you could swim!" But the time for the speech was not while he was under, right? When kids are drowning, you grab them.

Jesus pulled Peter out. "'You have so little faith,' Jesus said. 'Why did you doubt me?'" (v. 31). You see, the speech came after Peter was pulled out of the water. *"Why do you have so little faith? Why do you doubt Me? Don't you recognize I'm still standing on the water? Why did you doubt Me?"*

"When they climbed back into the boat, the wind stopped. Then the disciples worshiped him. 'You really are the Son of God!' they exclaimed" (vv. 32–33). The disciples all worshipped Jesus. They were like, *"You know, I was a little confused, Jesus, when You fed the five thousand starving people, but now that You've walked on water, I'm going to vote for you. You're the Son of God."*

God wants you to have faith. He wants all of us to have faith. But especially if you are a Six.

The Character of Sixes: They Reflect God's Faithfulness

Let's talk about Sixes. Sixes reflect God's faithfulness.

Don't you dare critique Peter. There were twelve disciples. How many got out of the boat? One. Why on earth would Jesus pick a Six to be the captain of the other eleven disciples? Because Sixes are loyal to the very end.

Peter always wanted to be faithful. He was afraid, but he was there. That's why Jesus turned to Peter and said, "I say to you that you are Peter (which means 'rock'), and upon this rock I will build my church, and all the powers of hell will not conquer it" (Matthew 16:18). He picked the one scared person to be the leader of the church. Why? Because it would require faith to do it. Sixes reflect God's faithfulness. Every time you criticize Peter, I want you to ask yourself this question: while Peter was screwing up, where were the other eleven? When Peter denied Jesus three times, where were the other guys? Not there. They weren't even there. Sixes are always there, because they reflect God's faithfulness.

The Core Motivation of Sixes: Safety

The primary motivation of Sixes is to be safe. Safety is what drives them and what motivates them.

If you're a Six, God has called you to great faith, but you will tend to lean toward great fear. When healthy, Sixes are able to determine character in the people they encounter. If you have a Six in your life, listen to their judgment of people. They see people better than you do.

I've learned this over and over again, the hard way, with my wife. I was in ministry with someone many years ago, of whom my wife said, "I don't like him. He gives me the heebie-jeebies. He gives me the creeps. I don't feel right around him."

I said, "Ah, you're just being sensitive."

Three months later that guy got caught sleeping with a woman who wasn't his wife. I should have listened to my Tammy; she sees people and reads them better than I do.

Why should you listen to a Six? They're reliable. They're loyal. Man, one of the things I love about Tammy is she has stuck with me. When I had nothing, she was with me. She never left me; she stayed by my side. She is trustworthy. She's compassionate and cares deeply about the church. She loves our church, she loves me, and she loves our kids.

Next, Sixes are good planners, which is why God had me marry a Six. When He gives me a vision such as, "We're going to plant five hundred churches," I ask, "How are we going to do it?" I don't know. God said, "*I'm going to give you a planner; she's going to help plan. She's going to be a part of organizing and making this happen.*" It's one thing to have a vision to build a rocket to the moon. It's another thing to get there.

Tammy is a great planner, and she's always planning. You should see her car. She has snacks in case something happens. She has money in case something happens. She has an earthquake preparedness kit. I'm always amazed at what she has; it's incredible. If you ever break down, don't worry; you're going to be okay. Tammy has snacks for you and is ready for whatever else may happen. If you break down with me alone, you're in trouble.

Fridays are my day off. As a Three, I work six days and reluctantly take one day off. One Friday Tammy said, "I want to go do a yoga class. Would you do me a favor and take Ethan to school today?"

I said, "No problem. I'll take him to school."

Now, here's what you need to know. I have a new car, and I don't exactly understand how it works because, remember, I don't read owner's manuals. So it's a new vehicle, and when we got into it, the car speaks to me in an Australian woman's accent. I picked it. I love it. She is so encouraging! "G'day, mate, you're low on gas. Would you like me to find a gas station for you?" I could press accept or ignore. So I ignored her. I'm a Three. *I'll tell you when we're out of gas.*

We started driving, and I took my son to school. I was just thinking about what I was going to do on my day off, when all of a sudden, I heard the car running out of gas. My old car would tell me, "You have twenty miles left . . . eighteen . . . ten . . ." all the way down to, "One mile left. Get gas!" My new car just gives you one verbal warning, and that's it. "G'day, mate, do you want to get gas?" No? All right, that's on you.

So I ran out of gas at 8:00 a.m. on a Friday. I had already dropped Ethan off, thank goodness, but I was not wearing a shirt. I had not combed my hair. I didn't have shoes on, I didn't have a phone, and I didn't have any money. What was I going to do? I pushed my car over to the side of the road and then tried to flag people down. Everybody was driving by, saying, "Kids, don't look, don't look." In Southern California, when you see a disheveled man with barely any clothes on heading in your direction, you look away—and motor!

Finally, some lady rolled her window down about two inches. She said, "You look like my son-in-law." We were talking through the crack in the window, and she said, "I'll call your wife for you." I give her the number, and she calls my wife. And of course, Tammy doesn't answer her phone. The woman said, "I have to go." She drove off and just left me there.

The next car came by, and it was a sheriff. I was saved! I was shirtless. I didn't have shoes on, and my hair looked like I'd been drinking all night. What could go wrong?

The sheriff got out of his car, I kid you not, and said, "How can I help you?"

I said, "Hey, man. I ran out of gas. My car is right back there. I just need a ride home. Can you give me a ride home?"

He said, "Yeah, sure. Hop in the back."

I had never, prior to that moment, been in the back of a police car. So there's a first time for everything. I was in the back of the police car, and we were cruising down the road. The sheriff was asking me where I live and punching it into his little computer. All of a sudden, he got an emergency call. He turned around and told me, "Sorry, you gotta get out."

He pulled the car over in front of a random house. He came around the side and got me out of the back of his police car. And, of course, people were outside doing yard work. So I waved at them: "Hi, guys!" Can you imagine if a police officer dropped off some shirtless, barefoot guy in your front yard? *Kids, get inside!*"

I was deciding what my options were. It was too far to run home, but I knew there was an elementary school on that street. Some of the teachers there go to our church, so without thinking about it, I ran to the school, walked into the school office, and asked to talk with a certain teacher.

All the office staff came out. "Why do you need to talk to her?"

"I need her car."

Thank God a member of my church was late bringing their

kids to school. She saw me and said, "I know him. He's my pastor. I'll take him home."

This will never happen to a Six. Their backup plans have backup plans. My wife never runs out of gas. And, thank God, she always drives with the appropriate amount of clothes on. Her motto is, "Don't be scared; be prepared." And I thank God for that. Sixes are loyal to you always. They're not questioning your judgment, doubting your vision, or trying to be a Negative Nancy. They just want to make sure we are all prepared in case things don't go as planned. And if you are in an adventure with a Three, things never go according to plan because they don't have one!

Healthy Sixes desire to see the world as a safer place. So if you have a friend who is a Six and you post a picture of your son skateboarding, they're going to say, "Where's the helmet?" That's just who they are. And that's good because that's safe. We want living kids.

The Core Sin of Sixes: Fear

When Sixes are unhealthy, they see only potential risk and danger. They are no longer planners but become avoiders. They only see the negatives. They have a hard time seeing the positives when they become unhealthy. Everyone's unsafe. Everyone is a risk, and they trust no one—often even the people who are closest to them. Their lives become dictated by fear and anxiety.

So what happened to Peter? When he was focused on the Lord, he had faith. What happened when he looked at the world around him, and he saw only risk and danger? He sank, and his life became dictated by fear and anxiety.

Look at American culture. Most of us are Sixes to some extent.

Our lives are dictated by fear and anxiety. Many of us are shut-ins, and we go nowhere.

When they're unhealthy, Sixes don't trust people. This causes them to avoid new experiences and to sabotage relationships, because when you believe that people are unsafe, you're going to cut off the relationship. You're going to cut them off before they cut you off. And you become your own self-fulfilling prophecy. So the core sin of the Six is fear. Fear can drive you to do crazy things, and it can drive you away from God.

The healthy Six is always in pursuit of courage—every day. They're asking themselves, *How am I going to be courageous today? How am I going to have courage in my marriage? How am I going to have courage at work? How am I going to have courage in my relationship with God? How am I going to have courage with my kids? How am I going to have courage with myself?* Healthy Sixes are always in pursuit of courage, trusting God, themselves, and eventually others. If you're a Six, know that God will get you there as you pursue health.

How Sixes Can Be Real with Self, Others, and God

How does the Six need to be real?

Real with Self

Sixes, I want you to focus on 1 Chronicles 28:20: "Be strong and courageous, and do the work. Don't be afraid or discouraged, for the LORD God, my God, is with you. He will not fail you or forsake you." Courage takes work. Every single day, when we face fear, we will choose to be courageous or we will choose to be afraid.

We all have a choice. "Be strong and courageous, and do the work." Things that matter most in life are worth fighting for, and you are not a thing—you are a child of God. You must learn to find your courage and take stands when you must. You don't have to worry about God; He is with you. You don't have to worry about storms. You just need to find your courage. It's in there. Some of the strongest people I have ever met are what's known as counterphobic Sixes. They attack what scares them. You can use this strength that's in you, even if you can't see any trace of it. It's in there because God put it in there! The good news just gets better; not only is the strength you need in you, the God who is loyal goes before you!

Deuteronomy 31:6 says, "Be strong and courageous! Do not be afraid and do not panic before them. For the LORD your God will personally go ahead of you. He will neither fail you nor abandon you."

God is already ahead of you. So take courage and chase after Him. You have got this because God has got you. Peter faltered, but Jesus remained steady. The apostle Paul, who was steady as a rock, reminds us in 2 Timothy 2:13 that "If we are unfaithful, he remains faithful, for he cannot deny who he is." Jesus didn't let Peter drown. He saved him at the very moment he lost faith. This is the God we worship. That is the God we love. He did not come to condemn us, but He came to save us.

When you're at your lowest, don't run from God; run to God because He loves you. He sent His Son to save you. No matter what's happening in your life, you need God. That's how you need to be real with yourself.

Real with Others

How do you need to be real with others? If you're a Six, look at the beauty of this verse: "Never let loyalty and kindness leave you!

Tie them around your neck as a reminder. Write them deep within your heart" (Proverbs 3:3).

We live in a world where people are often loyal to no one but themselves. If you're a Six, we need you. We need people who are loyal. They stick with it; they stay. If you are a Six, don't ever, ever give up on the gift God has given you. One of the things I love about my wife is that she has stayed with me throughout the years.

One weekend Tammy and I went to a leadership retreat at our church for our staff. And one of the young ladies in our church, who's now in her late thirties, got up and shared. I asked her, "How old were you when you started coming to Sandals Church?" She was eighteen years old, a college freshman. I've watched her go through college, get married, and have kids while being a part of our church. I said, "One of the things that I love is watching people who stuck with us through everything and have been loyal, and look at what God has done with her life." She's an inspiration.

Sixes, don't ever give up on the loyalty God has blessed you with. Don't ever let go of kindness. I don't care if everybody else doesn't have your gift; God gave it to you. Don't let it go. When you are loyal, you are like God. Be loyal.

If you're a Six, people are going to recognize your loyalty whether they acknowledge it publicly or not, and deep down in their hearts they wish they were more like you.

Real with God

Next, how can Sixes be real with God? Psalm 91:2 says, "This I declare about the LORD: He alone is my refuge, my place of safety; he is my God, and I trust him."

Why is this important if you're a Six? Because people will never be loyal to you in the way that you are to them.

One of the hardest things for my wife over the years has been watching people leave the church. I have to remind her over and over again, "God did not call us to follow them. He called us to follow Him. He is loyal." Sixes, you need to focus on God; stay with God. Some of your family will fall away. Some of your friends will fall away. You may have spouses and children who fall away. You must follow God despite what the world does, because He alone is your refuge. He alone is your place of safety. He is your God, and you can trust Him. Jesus promised that He would never leave us or forsake us. If you are a Six, don't read the second half of the verse, because it's a little scary—it says even if heaven and earth pass away. God is not trying to scare you; He is trying to comfort you. Jesus is loyal no matter what. Even when you die, as a Christian, it is the face of Jesus you will see, and He will say, *"I've still got you, I always have."* Remember, God is faithful to the core—that's who He is. Trust Him.

How Do You Love a Six?

So how do you love a Six? Please learn from my wounds.

1. Be secure and consistent.

When Tammy and I got married, I was neither secure nor consistent. Sixes hate the game musical chairs. I love it, but to them it's too unpredictable. So if you love a Six, you must become predictable and not make them feel like your relationship is an ever-changing game where you move the chair they need to sit in. Next, always tell the truth, no matter how painful it is. If you want to destabilize your life with a Six, lie to them. They may not have liked what you've done, but they will respect the truth you told. Always tell the truth—always. If you lie, you will have awakened that monster of fear that lives in their soul. And what it tells them is, "I can't trust anyone, including you." Sixes can handle almost any sin but lying.

2. Thank them for their loyalty to you.

Thank them just like I thank Tammy for her loyalty. Tell them, "Thank you for sticking with us through thick and thin. I am so grateful." I was a little slow on this until my pastor friend Mark challenged me. Mark is an Eight. We will talk about them later. But I was super thankful for him because I wasn't focused on how thankful I needed to be for Tammy. She is the center of our family unit and is afraid of everything and everyone but me. Over the years she has challenged me to not save the world and put our kids through hell. Thank you, Tammy. Thank your Six. They are a blessing.

3. Encourage them to be courageous.

Look, my wife's never going to be a big-wave surfer. She's not going to paddle out when the waves are big. But every now and then, she'll join me out in the ocean in waist-deep water. She'll come on out. Don't do what I used to do—freak her out. Don't do that. It feels funny, but it's not right. Celebrate it. Say, "Thank you so much for coming out and swimming in the ocean." And talk about how nobody died in the process.

You have no idea how hard it is for them to be courageous. My wife has a little note in our bedroom that says, "You've survived 100 percent of the days that have come before." So there's hope. My life is like, "What could go wrong?" My wife's life is like, "What could go right?" Thank Sixes for their loyalty, and encourage them to be courageous.

4. Fiercely support them when they're right.

We live in a world that has a hard time standing up for what's right. Sixes see the truth, and they bring us all to it. Support them when they're right. One of the weaknesses of Sixes is they have a hard time trusting the internal compass God has placed in their hearts. As a Three, I have a hard time caring if people think I am right; Tammy, as a Six, needs people to affirm that she is right. Remember, a Six is loyal to you, so you must be loyal when they are right or when they see something that is wrong. They have discernment about people, so trust them and support their discernment. Sixes can see what most of us miss.

5. Lovingly correct them when they're paranoid.

Sixes are going to be paranoid. A friend of mine is a pastor, and he's gone through some horrible things. There have been awful things written about him on the Internet. His family has been protested against, and they had to move. They have gone through all kinds of public drama.

So when he called, I never answered. Do you know why? Because his caller ID says, "Blocked Caller," and I have no idea who it is, so I never answer. He texted me, "Why didn't you answer?" I replied, "Because you're paranoid, and I didn't know it was you." I called him on it. "Look, not everyone is out to get you. Not everyone is unsafe. I have to be able to identify people when they call." Lovingly correct them when they're paranoid.

Sixes, your fear can get out of control. You're not going to drown when Jesus is standing there. It's not going to happen. When you teach your kids to swim, they panic and say, "I'm going to drown!" No, they won't, because you're at arm's length. You reassure them, "I've got you. I'm right here. I'm not going to let you go. I'm not going to let you drown. I care about you. I love you. It's okay. Just swim."

Sixes, it's okay. Jesus is here. You're not going to drown.

A Prayer for Sixes

Here's the prayer of the Six:

God, help me to be faithful to You. Help me to trust You even when people who speak for You are not trustworthy. Help me take courage every day. Help me rest in Your power and trust in Your goodness.

Life is cruel, and the world is not always good, but God is loving, kind, and faithful to the very end. Don't you dare confuse the world with God. They are not the same. Some of you are crippled by fear. Fear is owning you, and today's the day you need to let God own you. You need to let God take over, and you need to rid yourself of this fear. Take your attention off the waves, off the storm you're sinking in, and put your attention back on Jesus. Here is my prayer for you.

Heavenly Father, thank You for being a good and gracious God. Thank You for being trustworthy and loyal and kind. And in the moments when we are overwhelmed with fear, You are still with us. When we doubt, even when we lack faith—You are there. Help us not to listen to fear, because fear is a liar. Help us listen to You, because You are true. You are stable, and You are trustworthy. God, help us turn from fear and turn to You. We pray this in Jesus' name, amen.

type seven
<hr>

THE ENTHUSIAST

Joy vs. Avoidance

If you grew up Baptist, you might be a little uncomfortable with this chapter because it involves the word *dancing*. Right before I got married, my dad said, "You know why Baptists are opposed to sex?" And I said, "I don't know. Why, Dad?" He said, "Because it might lead to dancing." That's how serious they were about dancing.

Sevens in the Bible: King David

In 2 Samuel 6:14, look at what King David was doing: "David danced before the LORD with all his might."

Some of you can't lift your arms in worship. When you see people who worship with their arms lifted, you think they are getting a little too radical. "*Oh, put your arms down. Put your hands down.*" But in this chapter, we are talking about the Seven, the

Enthusiast. When Sevens worship God, there is usually body movement involved.

When I read that verse—"David danced before the LORD with all his might"—I think of the movie *Footloose*. It cracks me up. I've been married to Tammy for more than twenty-four years. We have two daughters, and they all love to watch the 1980s movie *Footloose*.

I had to explain to my girls and my wife, "When guys are frustrated or when they're really angry, they don't go out and dance." Right, guys? You have probably never, ever thought, *I am so mad, I am so ticked—give me my Walkman. I need to dance.* That's generally not how we work. It's funny to me how women think men are. I tell my daughters, "This is not how most men are. We are not like these guys in the movie."

But David "danced before the LORD." Who's David? David is one of the most important figures in the Bible. He's a man after God's own heart (1 Samuel 13:14). God selected him, and you need to know about his life: David was a great man who did great things, and he also did horrible things. But whatever he did, he did it with all his might no matter what direction he was going. He had fun— and screwed up his life and many others' lives.

But at that moment, in 2 Samuel 6:14, David "danced before the LORD with all his might, wearing a priestly garment." So this was like the pope in a mosh pit. And all the Catholics are like, *Oh no. It was funny when you made fun of the Baptists but not when you bring the pope into it.* Now you're uncomfortable. I'm just saying the Bible says David danced with all his might, and he was wearing a priestly garment. That's what Scripture says. If that makes you uncomfortable, be mad at God, okay? That's what it says.

The story continues, "So David and all the people of Israel brought up the Ark of the LORD with shouts of joy and the blowing of rams' horns" (v. 15). What's "the Ark of the Lord"? You don't know unless you've seen the Indiana Jones movies. It's kind of like that—but not like that at all.

The "Ark of the Lord" is a box. It's a box the Israelites carried that had the remnants of the Ten Commandments in it. And when the Israelites went to fight, the ark represented the presence of God with them. And when they led with it, no army could stand against them. That's why Indiana Jones had to steal it from Hitler!

Growing up as a Christian, I heard people in the church often say that you can't put God in a box, but in 2 Samuel, God was in a box! God was in this box, so to speak—the ark. The Israelites had it, and they were super excited about it. It's the presence of God. David is super excited, too, so "Israel brought up the Ark of the Lord with shouts of joy." Notice the verse says "shouts of joy." Some of you are going to be convicted about how you worship. The only thing you've ever shouted at is your TV when your favorite team is winning. That is when you praise. That's when you shout, right? Some of you are more passionate about your sports team than you are about Jesus, and you have to check yourself. When David worshipped the Lord, he got excited. He shouted with joy.

"Israel brought up the Ark of the Lord with shouts and the blowing of rams' horns" (v. 15). They had instruments. David would have played the electric guitar if he had one. But he didn't; he had a ram's horn, so that's what he had to work with. As the ark of the Lord entered the city of David, it was a party. But every party has a pooper, and that's why we invited . . . Michal. She is the daughter of King Saul (our undertalented but overly emotional Four from a couple of chapters back), and the wife of David, but here she plays the role of Debbie Downer. "But as the Ark of the Lord entered the City of David, Michal, the daughter of King Saul, looked down from her window. When she saw King David leaping and dancing before the LORD, she was filled with contempt for him" (v. 16). Remember, I said it was like *Footloose*. What was King David doing? He was "leaping and dancing before the LORD." And Michal "was filled with contempt for him."

It is amazing how critical we can be when other people cut loose and worship. We just stand there looking at them, thinking, *Is that really genuine?* Michal saw her husband, King David, leaping and dancing with all his might.

Wives, admit it: you've all seen your husbands doing something where you're like, "Ugh!" Guys, wives are like the rails in the bowling alley—you don't think you need them. You say, "I'm gonna bowl a 300." No, you're not! Get those rails on the lanes; they let you know when you're in the gutter.

Michal was looking at her husband, and she was embarrassed. Why? Because *Footloose* is embarrassing. It is. Unless you are Kevin Bacon. (Side note: people say I look like Kevin Bacon, but I cannot dance like him!) David was dancing, leaping before the Lord, and she was filled with contempt for him.

"They brought the Ark of the LORD and set it in its place inside the special tent David had prepared for it. And David sacrificed burnt offerings and peace offerings to the LORD. When he had finished his sacrifices, David blessed the people in the name of the LORD of Heaven's Armies. Then he gave to every Israelite man and woman in the crowd a loaf of bread, a cake of dates, and a cake of raisins" (vv. 17–19).

He had me until raisins. I think raisins are depressed grapes. There's an ongoing fight between my wife and me because she always buys raisins. They're never not in the cupboard. I don't even know when a raisin goes bad. The only thing raisins make better is bran!

"Then all the people returned to their homes. When David returned home to bless his own family, Michal, the daughter of Saul, came out to meet him" (v. 19–20). You know you're in trouble when your wife is in the driveway.

"She said in disgust, 'How distinguished the king of Israel looked today, shamelessly exposing himself to the servant girls like any vulgar person might do!'" (v. 20).

We don't know what happened, but at some point during the party, Christ-chela became Coachella, and clothing went flying. I guess that is what happens when you're leaping and dancing. You're not responsible for the linen flying off—it just happens. But she noticed.

"David retorted to Michal, 'I was dancing before the LORD, who chose me above your father and all his family!'" (v. 21). Things just got personal. Michal's father was Saul, the former king of Israel. He was our biblical character in the chapter on Fours!

"He appointed me as the leader of Israel, the people of the LORD, so I celebrate before the LORD. Yes, and I am willing to look even more foolish than this, even to be humiliated in my own eyes! But those servant girls you mentioned will indeed think I am distinguished!" (vv. 21–22).

David was saying, "*Look, when I worship God, things can get crazy. I might go a little nuts out there, but that's how God made me. That's who I am. And when I worship God, I do it with everything I have.*"

That's what the Enthusiast does. Whatever Sevens are doing, they're all in. They're all in all the time. When they are worshipping God, things get a lot out of control. The rest of us have to bring them back down. We are like, "Ooh, come back. It's okay. We love you. Put your clothes back on. We don't want to call the police."

The Character of Sevens: They Reflect God's Joy

So who is the Seven, the Enthusiast? Sevens reflect God's joy.

Have you ever been to a church service and you feel like God must hate us all? Tammy and I traveled to Europe and we visited some of those old churches. I made the mistake of going down to the break room where all the pastors congregate. They must have been eating raisins. Their faces looked like raisins. Have you been to a church and the pastor is grumpy and scowling, and he looks angry, yet he is saying, "I just love the Lord so much"? Oh yeah? Tell your face.

Sevens reflect God's joy. God is a God of joy. He loves to laugh. He loves to celebrate. This is who God is. When Jesus talked about judgment, He also talked about a party. You just choose which room you will spend eternity in—a cell or a celebration. Those are your options. You get to choose. God loves a good time. God loves to party. God loves to celebrate. He loves to do it in such a way that nobody gets hurt, pukes, or gets arrested. And Sevens reflect God's joy.

The Core Motivation of Sevens: Pleasure

What is the Seven's core motivation? What drives them? If you are a Seven, an Enthusiast, at the core of who you are—your internal motor—your motivation is pleasure.

God is the author of pleasure. We tend to act like pleasure is some horrible thing. A friend asks, "How was your time in Vegas?" And we respond, "Well, we were praying most of the time. We

gathered together to pray for all the heathens who are going to hell."
"Yes, but did you have a good time?" The friend didn't ask you, "Did
you sin?" How sad is it that when you do something really good—
like when you eat chocolate cake—we say it's "sinfully delicious"?

Do you know why the world says when something is good, it is
sinfully delicious? Because they've been to church and they didn't
see anything delicious! Instead, they say, "I'm never going back.
That was terrible."

The Seven's motivation is to find pleasure and to avoid pain.
The beauty of Sevens is that when healthy, they're able to bring or
to find joy in all situations. As a Seven, it doesn't matter how terrible
your job is; you will find a way to add joy into the mix.

When Sevens are unhealthy, pleasure dictates their life choices.
If you're a Seven, you have to be careful: just because it feels good
doesn't mean that you need to do it. That is what Sevens want to
do—whatever feels good.

Sevens also tend to be visionaries. Why would God choose a
Seven to lead Israel? Because God wanted him to have a vision.

Sevens are going to be different. They are not going to be like
everybody else. Sevens are versatile. Sevens can do many things. To
a Seven, it doesn't matter what you do. What matters is, can you
have fun? Can you find a way to have a good time? Sevens don't get
locked in. They just want to have a good time. They want to be with
people. They want to be on a team. They can lead the team, be on
the team, be the coach, or be on the bench. They don't care. They
are versatile. They don't get trapped in the idea of "I am what I do."

Sevens are resilient. They tend to be optimistic and positive.
They believe in things that people can't see. If you're negative, hang
out with a Seven. If you're a "glass half empty" type of person, you
need to be around somebody who's "glass half full" to level you out.

Sevens inspire people. Do you know what grade I got in my preaching class in seminary? I got an F. And F does not stand for fantastic. Do you know why I failed preaching? I failed because I didn't preach the way they said I should. I thought that was boring. I didn't think it worked, and I didn't think God's passion in my life was to put people to sleep. I don't want church to be the best nap of the week. I want to inspire people to live a better life, to live for God, and to make the world a better place. There's enough crappiness out there; we don't need to include church.

Sevens inspire people in projects. They say, "We can do this. We can make this happen." California has the least number of Christians of any state in the United States. People ask me all the time, "When are you moving to the Bible belt?" Never. Why do I want to go where there are already Christians? I want to reach lost people for Jesus because they need to know there's hope in this world, and there's goodness in Jesus.

Sevens Need to Be Free

If you're a Seven, an Enthusiast, or if you love someone who is, you need to know that Sevens fear a cage. They desire to be free.

In 2 Samuel 6, David decided to be free of clothing. Have you ever watched a little kid dance? They don't care. It's hilarious. You go to the beach, and they throw off their bathing suit—"I'm free!" If you're thirty, you're going to jail if you do that.

The Seven's core need is to be free. What's so sad is that everything about American culture is trying to put you in a box. Nobody puts Baby in a corner, as we learned in the 1987 movie *Dirty Dancing*, and no one should ever limit a Seven! Don't let people figure you out and force you into a box. As a Seven, you can do almost anything as long as it's fun.

Sevens Focus on Having Fun

When Sevens are healthy, they engage in fun. They like to have a good time. Sevens, don't apologize because you want to have fun. Don't say, "But I want to be taken seriously." Why? People make fun of my preaching all the time—"Well, he's just a comedian." Wait for it; I'm going to make you laugh and then punch you in your gut. My theory in preaching is to be funny, to give you a preacher punch, and then a hug. Spiritually speaking, I'm going to punch you with the truth, then give you a little hug and a laugh, and then I'm going to punch you again.

Sevens desire to make the world a more joy-filled place. Do we need more sadness? Is the world bankrupt of sorrow? Do we need more depression? Has anyone ever said, "I feel like this world is just so happy-go-lucky that I need to go to church to remind myself that life sucks"?

You might have picked up by now that Seven is my second highest number on the Enneagram assessment, behind Three. When my wife and I first got married, and we would go to a party, she would say, "Don't unleash all of Matt Brown. Be funny, but not too funny." She was a little nervous about what might happen, because when we pop the cork off that bottle, even I don't know what might happen. Sevens are able to bring joy in all situations.

Have you ever had a crappy job? I've had some bad jobs. One of the worst jobs I had was in the 1990s, and they were transferring everything from paper files to this technology called microfiche. We would take microscopic pictures of documents and shrink them so that the government could store all their information. It was a horrible job. That is what I did all day for eight hours a day. I used to announce to everybody, "We just made twenty cents!" "We just made thirty cents!" We had strict quotas. We had to take so many pictures on microfiche a day to keep our jobs. I never once met the quota, which got the attention of the owners of the company.

They called me in the owner's office, and I kid you not, we worked in a long building with one long hallway. I had to walk to the office all the way at the end. Everybody was like, "Oh, Matt's getting fired. We knew this would happen. He never makes quota." They ranked everybody according to efficiency on this chart every day, and I was always at the bottom.

So I was sitting in the owner's office, and he said, "You're the worst employee we have."

I said, "I know."

The owner said, "But this job sucks, and you make everybody want to come to work." They gave me a raise.

I walked out of there and said, "It's all right, everybody. I'm now making a nickel an hour more than you." That really happened. The owners knew it was awful, terrible work, and it was fun to have somebody there who could make light of a terrible situation.

Sevens are able to bring or find joy in all situations. Isn't it true? It's not just what you do, but who you work with. You could have a really cool job, but if everybody's terrible, you don't want to be there. You want to be somewhere else. It's not just what you do; it's who you have to do it with that matters. We want to do life with fun people, and Sevens are fun.

The Core Sin of Sevens: Gluttony

What's the core sin of the Seven? Gluttony. Doesn't that sound cool?

Sevens love a party. They don't care what it is. Have you ever eaten so much at Thanksgiving, you just had to repent? Every year

I say, "I'm not going to do that again. This year, Thanksgiving is really going to be about being thankful to God." How sad is that? The one holiday that's actually named Eucharist—that's what it is, Thanksgiving—and Sevens just pork out. And then they regret it because it hurts so bad.

That's what gluttony is. If one turkey leg is good, why not two? Why not three, why not four, right? If sex is good with one person, why not two, why not three, four, or five? Gluttony is a drive for more—whatever it is. It can binge on sex; it can binge on food; it can binge on Netflix. Sevens tend to say, "I'm going to watch the whole season, and I'm not going to sleep." They start watching. *"Oh my gosh, what time is it? Eleven p.m.? And it's Tuesday? I've been sitting here since Sunday."*

If you get to the bottom of the ice cream and you can't figure out why the spoon can't scrape through the container, this might be you.

Sevens Avoid Pain

Sevens usually want to escape pain at all costs. They run from pain. And I have news for you: the depth of pain you experience in life, I believe, is directly proportionate to your joy. It's one of the things that I think is going to make heaven so spectacular. We will know what joy is because we knew what pain was. You have to embrace the pain. Bad things happen to good people. You get fired, you get cancer, people die, and life doesn't make sense.

David ran from pain. He went through deep, deep pain, and every time he saw it, he ran from it. One of David's sons took sexual advantage of one of his daughters, and David did nothing. Nothing. He ran from it and ignored it. He didn't confront or challenge his son.

If you're a Seven, your job is not to make your kids your friends. You're supposed to be their parent. Your job is not to make your children like you. It's to try to raise them so when they're adults, people like them. You have to challenge bad behavior. You have to challenge immorality. You have to challenge your children, even if it hurts. Even in marriage, if you want a great marriage, you have to talk about the bad things, the ugly things, and the difficult things. If you want to destroy your marriage, Sevens, run from pain and sorrow—because eventually, it will find you. You can't outrun what's happened to you in your life. You deal with it, or it will deal with you.

Sevens often don't stay in a job very long. They move on from job to job to job, they move on from relationship to relationship to relationship, and they move on from friendship to friendship to friendship. Because as soon as it gets difficult, they're out.

I believe there's a reason God called me to be at one church my whole life. He knew it was the only way I would grow and change—by sitting in painful situations and dealing with them. Let me tell you something: I'm great at running, but I've had to learn that I can't outrun pain. Unhealthy Sevens can become impulsive and simply react. This is why if you're a Seven, you need Jesus. You need Jesus to guide you, to ground you, and to direct you. Sevens without God in their lives are like balloons in the air, floating in and out of storms. You need a rudder, you need a compass, and you need to be directed. When you're impulsive, you usually don't make a good decision.

If the words *what could go wrong* ever come out of your mouth— don't do it. If the reasoning behind the decision is, "What could go wrong?"—run. Sevens can become impulsive and just go after what they want.

In 2 Samuel 11, there's a naked woman taking a bath; her name is Bathsheba. *What could possibly go wrong?* I don't know, David. Then Bathsheba gets pregnant. What do you do, David? *"Um, I'll kill her husband."* And that is what David did. Uriah was a faithful soldier. He was faithful to David, committed to Israel, and devoted to God. David said to the commander of the army, *"Take Uriah to the front of the battlefield, and when the battle and the fighting is most fierce, I want you to pull back and leave him all by himself."* Uriah was killed. Even though David was the king of Israel and got away with that sin, guess who was watching? God. So God sent a prophet—an Eight!—by the name of Nathan to challenge David.

Sevens Fear Being Deprived

The core fear of the Seven is being deprived or trapped. The Seven has FOMO—Fear of Missing Out. They say, "I gotta be there. I can't miss the fun!"

If you're a Seven, guess what Instagram is saying? "You're missing out." Facebook says, "Oh, you should have been here. You're such a loser. It's too bad you didn't get invited." Too bad you actually have a real life with responsibilities, right?

Sevens can become impulsive and reckless. The definition of *reckless* is to act without thinking or caring about the consequences. How many hearts have been broken in the name of happiness?

You say, "Well, God would want me to be happy."

I say, "Show me that verse."

Happiness is found in God, and to pursue God we need to pursue righteousness. Holiness is a test, so we live in a world that's pursuing happiness. The evidence is all around. If you're under thirty, the world says have sex however you want, whenever you want, with whomever you want. In California, STDs are rising at a staggering rate.

Tammy and I were watching the news the other night. The reporter was talking, standing in front of a billboard. Because I have ADD, that means I wasn't listening. I was looking at everything else around the reporter.

I said, "Look at the billboard."

Everyone else in my family said, "What billboard?"

I said, "Look at that billboard behind him. Read it."

This guy was talking on the news about how one person got shot in California, so we should all be aware and lock our doors, and right behind him was a huge sign that said, "Syphilis is serious."

Young people, don't just lock your doors; lock your drawers. Syphilis is serious. But you're never going to hear that. We live in a world where there are no consequences; we can behave like nothing matters, and it's okay to behave irresponsibly. Parents, if you want to do your kids a favor, raise them knowing they have to grow up. I told my kids, "One day, I expect not to support you financially. That's the goal. Go out and work and support yourself and give back and contribute positively to society."

It's called adulthood.

How Sevens Can Be Real with Self, Others, and God

How can Sevens be real with themselves, with others, and with God?

Real with Self

The apostle Paul, who wrote half of the Christian Bible, wrote these words: "I have learned how to be content with whatever I have" (Philippians 4:11).

Sevens, the lie we tell ourselves is that doing the right thing will be a feeling we have one day. This is one of the reasons so many young people are finding it hard or impossible to support themselves, because they believe one day they'll feel like doing good. It's a miracle that most of us aren't homeless. It's not easy to get up and do things we don't want to do to provide for ourselves. It's hard.

Paul said, "I know how to live on almost nothing or with everything. I have learned the secret of living in every situation, whether it is with a full stomach or empty, with plenty or little" (v. 12). Here's the secret in every situation. Paul continued, "For I can do everything through Christ, who gives me strength" (v. 13). Paul was not talking about running a marathon or lifting weights. He was talking about getting through the day without coveting what everybody else has.

If you're a Seven, you have to learn to be content with what you have. Guess what robs you of the joy of what you have? Looking at what you don't have. Practice contentment by learning to reflect and to thank God for what He's done. Reflection is the key to contentment. Say, "Thank You, God, for what You've done. Thank You."

Often, my wife plans family nights. One family night we went to a theater in downtown Los Angeles and watched a reenactment of the movie *Beauty and the Beast*. It was fantastic. At one point, I'm going to be honest with you, I was crying, which, of course, my family found hilarious, right? I started crying when they sang the song that starts, "Tale as old at time . . ." That song is incredible, but what made me cry wasn't the production; it was remembering when my girls were little and watching them in their yellow dresses, dancing and singing every song in that movie. I wasn't regretting that they have grown. I was thankful that I got to be a part of it. I get to be their dad. My son is a teenager, and he slept through the whole thing. We paid eighty dollars for him to take a nap. Time is flying by, and most

Sevens' deepest fear is missing out. Well, if you spend your life chasing everything, you will have accomplished nothing. Remembering my little girls dancing, and missing the old days, was sad; not having those moments or memories would be devastating. Dads, moms, don't always go to the party. Stay home and dance with your little girls. Guys, at least once in a while, dance like Kevin Bacon!

Real with Others

How can Sevens be real with others? In 1 Samuel 18, King Saul's son Jonathan—who I believe was a Six, the loyal friend—made David reaffirm his vow of friendship. Why? Because David was flighty; he was a Seven. Sevens, if they're not careful, can be a mile wide and an inch deep. Then Jonathan made David reaffirm his vow of friendship again. Why? Because David was a Seven. Jonathan loved David as he loved himself. Jonathan was a loyal friend to David, but he had to make David recommit. Sevens, not everything is about fun. Some things are difficult, some things are hard, and the most beautiful friendships are the ones that last.

As a Seven, you can't just pursue good times; you need to pursue good people. You need to learn to be loyal to people. As a Seven people will love you and be drawn to you. Your challenge will never be attracting people; it will be to be good to people. But you don't just need good people, you need strong people who love you enough to challenge you. Jonathan wasn't just a good friend to David; he was a great friend. Jonathan wasn't afraid to stand up for what was right. Jonathan was a warrior, but he also had character. Jonathan had some type One in him. If you are a Seven, find a One who loves you enough to call you on your crap. As a Seven, you need truth-tellers, because the problem for the Seven is always that they don't know what the problem is. Ones do, and they will tell you.

Real with God

How can you be real with God if you're a Seven? Psalm 16:11 says, "You will show me the way of life, granting me the joy of your presence and the pleasures of living with you forever." God is the author of pleasure, and He has offered for you to spend eternity with Him.

Remember how David partied? He danced before the Lord! Why? Because there is no greater joy than serving the author of joy. Sevens are naturally spirited people. As a Seven you don't need more spirit, but you do need more of the Holy Spirit. The Holy Spirit can keep up with you, because you can't outrun God's Spirit.

David learned this firsthand when he said, "Where can I go from your Spirit? Where can I flee from your presence?" (Psalm 139:7 NIV). David had tried to outrun God's Spirit, but no matter where David went, God's Spirit was there. As Sevens, you will flee from pain. Notice David asked where he could flee. Stop running from God's Spirit and invite Him to take control of your boundless energy and joy for life.

Galatians 5:22 states, "The Holy Spirit produces this kind of fruit in our lives: love, joy . . ." Who said God doesn't want you to be happy? As a Seven, you just haven't learned what it is yet. When God gives His love and His joy, He will give you supernatural self-control so you can begin to say no to your desires and yes to God's.

How Do You Love a Seven?

How do you love the Sevens in your life?

1. Give them lots of room to play and really have fun.

A couple of years ago, my son was in trouble at school. He is a boy, is a high Seven, and has lots of energy. So I went up to his school. Boys often have a harder time than girls sitting still and struggle with paying attention, and we label many of them as having ADHD, but I think some boys just have high Seven gifting. I was sitting in a room with his teachers, I'm guessing they were all Ones, perhaps a tad unhealthy. I said my son is just a boy with lots of energy. One of the female teachers said, "I have studied boys." And maybe she had, but her counsel was to take away recess—the only part of school my son likes. Sevens usually have a hard time sitting still. Sevens have a hard time caring about Pharaoh and how many stones it took to build a pyramid, which is what my son was supposed to be learning, but they do care about how many minutes there are at recess. Let Sevens play. They need it!

2. Recognize when they choose to deal with problems.

Don't say to a Seven, "It's about time." Don't say, "It's about time, David, that you got real with your stripping naked problem."

Recognize how hard it is for them to face their pain and deal with the problem. Figure out a way to support them as they deal with their pain. Unfortunately for David, he never learned how to deal with his pain. And his family constantly paid the consequences. Maybe say something like, "Wow, I am so proud of the fact that you are talking about this! I can't imagine how hard this is for you. How can I come alongside you to help you deal with this now so that we don't have to deal with it again later?"

3. Share how much joy they bring to your life.

If you throw lousy parties, invite a Seven. And when the Seven asks, "What are we going to do?" you say, "Whatever you usually do—as long as it's not immoral or illegal and the police don't show up." Then join in the fun. Have a good time—live a little. Even if you are a One, Two, Five, or Six! Life is serious enough, and we have to learn to relax. We sweat things that just don't matter. We make big deals of little things. Whatever it is, get over yourself and learn to have a good time and join the event.

How different the story would have been if Michal had jumped down there and started dancing too. Perhaps they would have had a better marriage if she could have loosened up a little bit and danced and praised the Lord with her husband, rather than making fun of his desire to enjoy life.

A Prayer for Sevens

Here's a prayer for the Sevens to pray:

> *God, help me run to You and not from the pain or toward all pleasure. Help me develop deep and lasting friendships with people who want to have fun but can keep me grounded. Help me have the tough conversations real life requires, and remind me to be thankful for what You have done.*

Sevens, you brighten our days, but make sure you're following Jesus, or the party will end when your life is over. Make sure you make it to the big party—and the only way you do that is through faith in Jesus Christ. Here is my prayer for you.

> *Father God, we are so thankful and grateful for the Sevens, the Enthusiasts, in our lives. We're thankful for these people who make even mundane jobs fun. They bring joy to boring business meetings and all the things we do. God, help us love*

them and celebrate them. And help the Sevens not just live for pleasure but live for You. Help them not run from pain but embrace it as a part of life. Bless us all with a desire to be real and to follow You. We pray this in Jesus' name, amen.

THE CHALLENGER

Power vs. Lust

I f you're an Eight, just know that we love you, we care for you, and we need you. People who score an Eight on the Enneagram assessment may say, "Oh no—I'm the person everybody is afraid of or intimidated by." I just want you to know that God made and designed you, and you are amazing. God wants to use you in the healthy category of Eight. In this chapter, we are going to talk about Eights and see why we need the Challengers.

Eights in the Bible: Nathan

There are many, many Eights in the Bible, and God uses them to do incredible things. In the previous chapter, we talked about a Seven, David, who was an Enthusiast. David was excited, and he danced before the Lord. Unfortunately, he got a little too excited about a married woman named Bathsheba. He slept with Bathsheba, and she became pregnant. He had to figure out how to fix that problem, because he was the king of Israel and he had impregnated a married woman. This woman's husband was off fighting for David's kingdom on the battlefield. The Bible is very clear that David did a lot of nasty things. He was impulsive, reckless, and had a hard time trying to cover up his sin.

The first thing David did to try to cover his sin was to invite Bathsheba's husband, Uriah the Hittite, back from the battlefield. He said to Uriah, "We appreciate all your faithfulness and loyalty, but we want you to come back and have some R&R with your wife." Uriah was a good guy, and he refused to go home to sleep with his wife. Instead, he thought about his buddies and fellow soldiers out on the battlefield. They were not with their wives. They didn't get to sleep at home. So he decided to sleep outside in a tent, in honor of his comrades out on the field.

Then David tried something else. He invited Uriah to the palace and got him drunk. He hoped Uriah would go back and sleep with his wife, but Uriah still wouldn't do it. David was in a conundrum. But instead of doing the right thing and confessing his sin, he gave Uriah a note and said, *"Take this to Joab when you go back on the battlefield."* The note said, *"Put Uriah up front and make sure he dies."* How terrible is that? David arranged to kill this loyal man of his kingdom in order to cover his own sin. So Uriah died on the battlefield, and David felt like everything was fine. He thought he got away with it.

Here's the thing you need to know about sin. You might fool your pastor. You might fool the police. You might fool your friends. But you cannot fool God.

So God ordained an Eight, a Challenger named Nathan, to come into the situation and challenge David for his sin.

In 2 Samuel 12:1, the narrative begins: "So the LORD sent Nathan the prophet to tell David this story." Nathan, a very healthy Eight, had some nuances to his confrontation style.

Nathan told this story to David:

> There were two men in a certain town. One was rich, and one was poor. The rich man owned a great many sheep and cattle. The poor man owned nothing but one little lamb he had bought. He raised that little lamb, and it grew up with his children. It ate from the man's own plate and drank from his cup. He cuddled it in his arms like a baby daughter. One day a guest arrived at the home of the rich man. But instead of killing an animal from his own flock or herd, he took the poor man's lamb and killed it and prepared it for his guest. (vv. 1–4)

"David was furious" (v. 5). This was ridiculous. Who would have done something like this to the poor man? "'As surely as the LORD lives,' he vowed, 'any man who would do such a thing deserves to die! He must repay four lambs to the poor man for the one he stole and for having no pity'" (vv. 5–6). This is a little over the top, which Sevens can be. You don't give somebody the death penalty because they killed your pet. Maybe they should be put in prison or given some counseling. But you don't put someone to death because they killed your dog. David lost his mind and said that the rich man must be punished because he had no pity.

This next verse is one of the greatest moments in Scripture: "Then Nathan said to David, 'You are that man!'" (v. 7). David was very serious and fired up. He wanted the rich man to die. Then

Nathan said, *"You're that guy."* It was even more dramatic than the "You can't handle the truth!" scene in the movie *A Few Good Men.* Nathan continued:

> The LORD, the God of Israel, says: I anointed you king of Israel and saved you from the power of Saul. I gave you your master's house and his wives and the kingdoms of Israel and Judah. And if that had not been enough, I would have given you much, much more. Why, then, have you despised the word of the LORD and done this horrible deed? For you have murdered Uriah the Hittite with the sword of the Ammonites and stolen his wife. From this time on, your family will live by the sword because you have despised me by taking Uriah's wife to be your own. (vv. 7–10)

Then David confessed to Nathan that he had sinned against the Lord. You have to love Sevens when they get it. Nathan said, "Yes, but the LORD has forgiven you, and you won't die for this sin" (v. 13). This is one of the greatest showdowns in the Bible. This is like the gunfight at the O.K. Corral in Tombstone, Arizona. The king of Israel in all his might and all his power against Nathan, the Challenger.

The Character of Eights: They Reflect God's Power

So if you're an Eight or you know somebody who is an Eight, remember this: Eights reflect God's power.

Now, some of you are raising little Eights. They defy you; they challenge you, and they push against you. Don't give up, and don't give in. Know that God has made them powerful for a reason. They're Challengers. They challenge rules, and they challenge your thinking and ideas. They challenge education. They challenge everything. This is how God has wired them.

The Core Motivation of Eights: Power

The core motivation for Eights is power. Eights naturally and instantly assess the room to see who the most powerful person is. When healthy, Eights acknowledge this person and figure out whether or not they can follow him or her. When unhealthy, Eights have to see who is stronger and more powerful. It cracks me up when I walk into a room with other megachurch pastors. These are pastors who operate with congregations of thousands of people. When I walk in and look around, there's a lot of posturing going on. We're all Christian pastors, but everyone is measuring and checking each other out to see who's the most powerful person in the room.

When healthy, Eights are strong and confident. In our world today, where people often don't know what they want to do or what they want to be, Eights know what they want to do, and they know what they need you to do. They're very clear. They're strong, and they're confident. They are not wishy-washy. They are not moved by the ever-changing current of culture because they know who they are and what they're about.

Eights Need to Be in Control

The core need of the Eight is to be in control. Now, you might be saying, *This is not me. I thought I was an Eight until this point.*

Let's look at this a different way. Maybe you wouldn't say that you want to be in control. However, what if I said this: *you don't want to be controlled.* I think that's an easier way to explain it for many Eights. And just so you know, Eight is the third highest score on my Enneagram assessment. Often, my wife and I will have conflict when I feel like she's trying to control me. It usually happens when it feels like she's trying to mother me or give me some advice. For example, if she points out directions to me on the way home, I think, *I drive home every single day. Why is she trying to control the way I drive?* My Eight comes out because I don't want to be controlled. Part of that is my high Seven need to be free. The Eight sees the world as: "Who is in control? Is it me or is it someone else?"

Now, if Eights respect and believe in you, they may follow you. If they do, they are going to be okay. There are healthy Eights who work for me, and they're great. They trust me and believe in the vision of our church. This team of God is very powerful. However, when Eights are unhealthy, anytime you try to correct them or advise them, they feel that you're trying to control them. They feel like you're trying to tell them what to do, and they'll push back against that. So if you're an Eight, really look at yourself and be honest. Ask yourself, *Is this an issue in my life?*

Often Eights are unhealthy because when they were kids, their voices weren't heard. Their opinions didn't matter. Everything that they did was controlled or micromanaged. So they see adulthood as a way to escape from the bonds of parenting and control. Your strategies as a child work as a child. However, when you become an adult, they won't work at all. As a matter of fact, what protected you as a kid will actually destroy you as an adult. So you need to take a step back and say, "I'm not in that home anymore. I didn't marry my mom. I'm not in a relationship with my dad. My kids are very different. My boss is different." You have to understand that one of the things that can wreck your future is your past. So you have to deal with your past, accept it, and move forward.

Eights are not led by the heart or the head, but by instinct. Like Nines and Ones, they instinctively know what's right and what's wrong. They have an internal compass, and they know what they need to do. They don't need your meetings—they just need to fix the problem. And if you get in the way, you're part of the problem.

Eights Focus on Justice

Healthy Eights want the world to be more just. We need more justice in this world. We need people who will stand up for the people who don't have a voice. Nathan proudly stood up for Uriah; he gave a voice to the one who had lost his voice. We need them to stand up for the people who are not heard.

One great Eight in our culture was Martin Luther King Jr. The reverend was an Eight. He basically said that black people were not being treated fairly. He instinctively knew that this was wrong and unjust, so he stood up to the most powerful nation on earth and said that we need to treat people equally. The Rev. King was peaceful but powerful. Another Eight was Winston Churchill. Hitler had destroyed nearly all of Europe. Europe was bowing down under the power and the weaponry of Nazi Germany. England was almost totally defeated and broken down. They had no chance and no hope. Churchill, who was a healthy Eight, said these beautiful, powerful words in a speech to the House of Commons on June 4, 1940: "We shall fight on the seas and oceans, we shall fight with growing confidence and growing strength in the air, we shall defend our Island, whatever the cost may be, we shall fight on the beaches, we shall fight on the landing grounds, we shall fight in the fields and in the streets, we shall fight in the hills; we shall never surrender."[1] With that, he galvanized the nation. Not only that, but he inspired the United States. At that time, the US was wavering on what to do. As a healthy Eight, Churchill inspired us to get involved and stand up for what was right, just, and true.

Here's the thing you need to know about Eights. Eights communicate directly. Nathan said, "You are that man!" David didn't take some man's little lamb. He stole a man's wife. Even though David had many wives and concubines, he still took another man's wife. You may have missed this in the Bible story. Just as Martin Luther King Jr. talked about how blacks and whites were treated differently, David did the same thing. Uriah was not Jewish; he was a Hittite. He was from another nation and another land. Since Uriah was a foreigner from another country, David apparently believed he had permission to treat Uriah differently. Nathan, however, clearly believed that God cares about all people.

Next, when healthy, Eights lead and influence others to get things done. They do great things. They can take businesses or colleges from the brink of disaster and bankruptcy and turn them around. Steve Jobs is another great Eight. He started Apple Inc., but he became an unhealthy Eight. He did some questionable things, and they kicked him out. Then, eventually, Apple brought Steve Jobs back, and he galvanized them. One of my favorite speeches he gave was when he came back to Apple and addressed all the engineers, asking this question: What's wrong with Apple? Everybody started murmuring, and he said, "It's the products! So what's wrong with the products? The products suck!"[2] He continued to explain what was wrong and what had happened. It takes leaders like that to speak directly and influence others to get things done. That's what I love about Eights. They don't beat around the bush. They're direct and very clear. They find the problem, figure out what needs to be done, and change things.

Next, Eights are protective of those they see as vulnerable. Just as Nathan spoke up for the Hittite, Martin Luther King Jr. spoke up for blacks in America. Winston Churchill spoke up for the free world. These men were fighting against evil, and they were protective of those they saw as vulnerable. Often, Eights are compared to eggs. They have a hard shell on the outside, but they're mushy on the inside. They have a soft spot for people they see as vulnerable. Eights are God's gift to us to protect those of us who aren't powerful or strong and who don't have a voice. So a healthy Eight is always in pursuit of tenderness and mercy. This is key if you're an Eight. If you're a healthy Eight, you're going to be tender and merciful.

One of my kids is a strong Eight. I'm constantly saying, "Be tender and be soft." This is because kids who are Eights are going to have a hard time with things like petting the dog. They're going to grab the dog and move the dog wherever they want. So I say, "Be tender. Be soft. Don't hurt the dog. Be gentle." And that's just how Eights are. They're strong individuals, so they have to pursue tenderness and mercy.

Now, what happens when you're an Eight and you shift to the unhealthy side? We see how God used Nathan, the prophet, to speak truth into David. When unhealthy, Eights use their power to dominate others and to get things done their way. David probably had some Eight in him. If he could have taken the Enneagram assessment, he probably would have had high Eight or maybe Seven-wing-Eight in him. When David used his power, he used it to dominate and get what he wanted. That included killing Uriah the Hittite, who had been faithful to him. So as an Eight, you have to be really careful that you don't use your power for your gain. You have to use it for good things, like mercy and tenderness. You have to use it for people who don't have a voice.

When Eights are unhealthy, they are forceful, insensitive, and don't care about anyone's feelings. They care about getting things done. If you have a boss who's unhealthy, he or she is going to yell at you because you didn't meet the deadline. This person doesn't care how you feel. All your boss cares about is getting the job done. Eights are naturally combative. They don't mind a little blood, but when unhealthy, they look forward to this and thrive on it. They think, *Who am I going to fight today?*

Next, I don't say this to be mean, but unhealthy Eights are relationally clueless. They don't see how their personality, words, and decisions affect everybody else. To them, nobody else exists in the room, because they want to do what they know is right. Everybody can be crying or upset, and Eights don't see it at all. Since they're relationally clueless, they miss the subtle nuances of people's expressions. For example, if an Eight tells me he or she is going to do something, and I have a certain expression on my face, an Eight doesn't read that. An Eight is not looking at my face. He or she is not responding to anything other than his or her decision and what the Eight wants done. So if you love somebody who's an Eight, don't take this personally. It's just a blind side of an Eight's personality. Eights do not see the subtle nuances of how people respond and how people work together in social situations. When unhealthy, Eights tend to be blind to how people are perceiving them and receiving them.

Next, when Eights are unhealthy, they don't see the value of other people's opinions. To Eights, it doesn't matter what other people think. They don't want to go to any meetings because they already know they're right. They feel that other opinions are ridiculous, and the world would be a better place if everybody just did what they did. Eights are convinced that if everybody would follow them, listen to them, and drive like them, every problem would be solved. They don't see the value of others' opinions and they don't experience the opinions of others. They just don't understand why people don't see their answers. And that's how they live.

The Core Sin of Eights: Lust

Let's talk about the core sin of an Eight. If you're an Eight, this is going to be a little difficult to share in small group and maybe a little awkward to bring up when you're among your friends. I'm going to explain what this means, so don't freak out. The core sin of the Eight is lust. Yes, it can be sexual.

An Eight in the Bible who I think struggled with lust immensely was Samson. Samson was an incredibly powerful guy and stronger than everybody else. He was literally filled with the Spirit of God to do all kinds of things. However, he was also clueless. His sexual appetite and sexual desire made him blind. All he saw was himself and his own desires. Ultimately, his lust for a woman named Delilah brought him down. When you read the story in Judges 16, you're probably wondering what it is going to take for him to see Delilah for who she is. She's already tried to kill Samson multiple times, but he can't see past his own sexual desire. So that's how lust for sex can bring an Eight down. However, it is usually a lust for power. It's an insatiable appetite to be in control or to attain authority. As I said earlier, when an Eight walks into the room, they're going to measure everybody up. Who is the strongest? Who is the most powerful? Who is the person in the room who gets things done? When Eights are unhealthy, they have a desire to be in control and to be in power.

Eights Avoid Vulnerability

Eights avoid being vulnerable at any cost. They don't want to share what's going on. They act like they don't have feelings or emotions. They're just getting things done and plowing through life.

However, the reality is that Eights are humans too. They have feelings. They have hearts. They just don't want to let anybody in. For people who are married to Eights, this is going to be really challenging. If they're unhealthy, it will be difficult to find out how they feel. It will be difficult to know what they're thinking because Eights tend to put up walls, which doesn't allow them to be real. They can be forceful, insensitive, or combative. For Sampson, he was not real until the end of his life; he ended up blind and broken. When his emotional walls finally came down, it killed him and everyone around him. Don't wait until the end of your life to be vulnerable. Don't wait until the end of your life to get real. Sampson had lots of sex, but he never experienced intimacy.

Eights Fear Being Exposed

Here's the core fear of the Eight: they do not want to be exposed. This means Eights probably won't want to go to a small group. Eights don't want to get real. They probably view a small group as a self-help group where they would have to get emotional or watch others doing this.

I remember the first time I was in a small group with an Eight. That person left in the middle of our meeting. He was done and just bolted. This made everybody uncomfortable. It was weird, but at the time I didn't have the language to speak to him because he was not interested in being real—and I did not have the skills to help him. He thought we were going to study the Bible and what's right, good, and true. As soon as the discussion went into feelings, he got his wife and their kids and left. They never came back. That's what happens when Eights are unhealthy. They don't want to be exposed or real.

How Eights Can Be Real with Self, Others, and God

How does the Eight, the Challenger, need to be real?

Real with Self

If you're an Eight, you have to deal with the mush. You have to deal with feelings. Let's be honest: none of us wants to be exposed. It's vulnerable. It feels awkward. It's very scary, because we've been hurt by people in our past. When we did share our feelings, people didn't handle it well. I get it.

So here's how Eights need to be real with themselves. James 2:13 says, "There will be no mercy for those who have not shown mercy to others." God is very declarative. If you're an Eight, this verse is just in your face. You're not going to receive mercy if you don't give mercy to others. You don't get extra-credit points for being harsh. You get extra-credit points for being tender, having mercy, and being compassionate. There will be no mercy for those who have not shown mercy.

Even when David was confronted by Nathan, God showed mercy when David did not deserve mercy. Remember what David said needed to happen to the man who stole the lamb? He said, "As surely as the LORD lives, any man who would do such a thing must die!" (2 Samuel 12:5). Well, God didn't kill David. He didn't destroy him. God showed mercy on David, who showed no mercy to Uriah the Hittite. That's the reality for all of us. We don't deserve God's mercy, but He gives it to us anyway. Our job is to give it to others, especially if we're an Eight. "There will be no mercy for those who have not shown mercy to others."

However, if you have been merciful, God will be merciful when He judges you. Every single one of us will stand before God and be judged for the way we lived. A lot of Christians are confused about Romans 8:1, which says, "There is no condemnation for those who belong to Christ Jesus." To be condemned is to die. You are not going to die because of your sins before God, but you will stand before God and be judged. Every single one of us will stand before the almighty God and be judged. Those of us who belong to Christ won't be condemned. Those who do not belong to Christ will receive condemnation. This is the due penalty for our sins. So don't confuse that word. You will not be condemned; however, you will be judged. You will be held accountable for your sins, just as David was.

David didn't die, but here's what happened: God took all his wives. He said, "*I would have given you everything. I would have blessed you. I raised you up from nothing and gave you this power and strength.*" Instead, God said, "I will give your wives to another man before your very eyes, and he will go to bed with them in public view. You did it secretly, but I will make this happen to you openly in the sight of all Israel" (2 Samuel 12:11–12). God said, "*Because you destroyed Uriah's family, I'm going to destroy your family. Since you took one man's wife, I'll take all your wives.*" So there was judgment. God was merciful, but David was still judged. David's family life from that point forward was anything but blessed. It was a disaster.

This does not need to be you. You can change. One of my best friends in the entire world is an Eight. He struggles sharing his feelings, and he struggles with intimacy and mush! Years ago I handed him jagged rocks and told him to ask God what they meant for him.

Months later he came to me, frustrated, and said he had no idea what the jagged rocks meant. I told him that they represented him, and God wanted them to become smooth. The only way rocks become smooth is when they are repeatedly pounded against other rocks. Over the years we have clashed but have both become smoother and better people because of each other's God-given personalities. If you're an Eight, God doesn't want you to be any less of a rock—he just wants to smooth your rough edges!

Real with Others

How do Eights need to be real with others? This is going to be a lifelong challenge. If you're an Eight, you're going to be stronger than everybody else. You're going to be more powerful than everybody else, and people are going to be intimidated by you. So you have to really press into this if you want to be healthy.

James 3:17 says, "The wisdom from above is first of all pure. It is also peace loving, gentle at all times, and willing to yield to others. It is full of mercy." I want you to pay attention to these words: "willing to yield to others." Here's the thing about Eights. Unhealthy Eights say, "I want to be in charge. I want to be an authority." And without accountability, they don't last. At the church where I serve as pastor, we have a whole board who holds me accountable. I'm accountable to our pastors. I'm more accountable than anybody I know. I open my life up for people to speak into on a regular basis. Healthy Eights are willing to yield to others. They're willing to yield to people they respect, trust, and admire.

As an Eight, you have to find somebody you're willing to submit to. You have to find somebody who you're willing to follow. If you can't do that, you can't be a Christian, because Christians have to submit to Jesus. You have to follow Jesus. An unhealthy Eight says, "It's my way or the highway." A healthy Eight says, "Here's my opinion. Here's what I think we should do. However, I am willing to listen to others, and my prayer is that the best decision wins." The Eights usually think the best decision is their decision, but sometimes it's somebody else's decision or somebody else's idea.

Eights, you have to have mercy for the people in your life. You just do. There are a lot of people in your life who might seem ignorant or ill-informed to you. Your job is not to lead and control them. Your job is to love them. Your job is to care for them and to lead them, out of respect for what God has called you to do. He's given you His power and strength. You need to use it for Christ and not for yourself.

Real with God

How can you be real with God as an Eight? I love 2 Corinthians 12:10, which says, "That's why I take pleasure in my weaknesses, and in the insults, hardships, persecutions, and troubles that I suffer for Christ. For when I am weak, then I am strong." If you've ever heard me speak, you probably noticed that I don't share about how I *almost* sinned. I share about how I *really* and *recently* sinned. People are not drawn to stories of you almost blowing it. When people hear me talk, they don't think, *I could never be like that guy.* No, they think, *Wow! If God can use a knucklehead like him, there is hope for me!* People will be intimidated by your strength, but they will be drawn to your honesty about being weak. We are all stronger when we share our weaknesses.

Eights, you're not perfect. You're not a robot. You're going to make mistakes, and you need to be vulnerable. You need to share your weaknesses. It's in those moments that you're strong—because weakness makes us dependent on God. That is the beauty of weakness. When I'm leaning on God, I'm strong and powerful. When I'm leaning on my own strength, I can only do what I do. When I lean on God, I can do what He does.

An Eight has to constantly come to God with a humble attitude and with a broken spirit. He or she needs to say, "Lord, I need You." Be willing to share your mistakes and weaknesses. Be willing to share your fears, because I have to tell you something: if you're an Eight, no one in your community group thinks you have never had a fear. Even though you come off as not afraid of anything, the reality is you are terrified. You are terrified, first and foremost, of sharing your feelings. Share that. Be honest about it. Talk about how hard it is for you to share. A lot of times, Eights don't think they have any sins. You do. You're stronger than everybody else, but you're not better than everybody else. So share your weaknesses. Start with God. As 1 John 1:9 says, "If we confess our sins to him, he is faithful and just to forgive us our sins and to cleanse us from all wickedness." If we claim that we have no sin, we are only fooling ourselves and calling God a liar. If you're an Eight and you don't think you're broken and a mess, you are calling God a liar. God is not a liar. He is truthful. The Bible says, "Everyone has sinned; we all fall short of God's glorious standard" (Romans 3:23). All of us sin, including the Eight.

How Do You Love an Eight?

How on earth do you love an Eight? This is something that I've had to learn. I've struggled with Eights. Eight is my third highest score. My wife says that I save all my unhealthy Eight for her, and I blow up and get angry. However, my highest score is a Three, then Seven. So I do have some Eight in me, but it's not all of who I am. I can, however, give you some tips on how to love an Eight.

1. Notice when they're tender.

Notice when they're compassionate. Notice when they're sweet. Notice it and say, "Thank you for doing that." However, here's the thing with Eights: You don't have to flatter them. They don't want compliments. They don't want a bunch of lip service. Just say, "Hey, thank you so much for being that way." The key with an Eight is to be direct, concise, and crystal clear.

2. Speak directly.

Don't waste their time. Eights don't need a bunch of words. They need to know how you feel. One of the things that I love about 2 Samuel 12 is that Nathan explained what was going to happen. He said, *"God's going to judge you. He's not going to kill you, but here's all the terrible things that are going to happen to your family."* Then Nathan left. He said what he needed to say, and then he left. He didn't need to be David's counselor. He was not going to be his soul-care person. Nathan delivered God's message, and his job was done. So that's how you speak to an Eight. Be direct. Don't be all over the place. Speak directly to the person. This has been hard for me because I like nuance when people speak to me. I'm a Three, so I like a little flattery. I like to hear things like, "Oh, you're so amazing." Eights don't like that. They want to hear, "Here's what I need you to do. Here's what I want." Eights do really well in the military because they take orders, and then they go out and make it happen. So when you're talking to Eights, speak directly to them and don't mess around. Just get to the truth and say, "Here's what I want you to do." You have to be declarative with an Eight.

3. Stand up for yourself.

You cannot leave any room at all for Eights to think that maybe you weren't clear. Just so you know, Threes tend to withhold truth because we're afraid of hurting people's feelings. If you do that with an Eight, they will not understand what you mean. You have to say something like, "Here's the decision. This is how it's going to be, and I'm not changing." You have to be clear. If you're raising an Eight, you say to that child, "Here's how it is. If you don't like it, then too bad. We're not changing." This is because Eights are going to challenge the rules, and you have to stand up for yourself. Here's how you earn respect from people who are Eights: stand up for them when they're right. People may not like it, but a lot of times your Eight is right. So you stand up for them. You say, "I may not agree with how they said it, but the reality is, they're right."

Eights need to get to work on being more real with whatever they are confronting people about. They need to read their Bibles or other resources that can help them, because they don't always hold people's hearts well. Nathan was not really interested in David's heart; he was interested in calling out his sin. So he spoke to that. The Word of God agreed with Nathan that what David did was wrong. With Eights, it's better to talk about their approach rather than whether or not what they're saying is right.

4. Don't assume they meant to be hurtful.

When Eights speak directly, they're simply trying to be clear. This tends to hurt other people's feelings. Don't assume that was their intent. Here's the thing I try to talk about when it comes to Eights: remember their heart, remember their calling, and remember their passion. Something you have to understand about Eights is that God made them strong. He made them powerful. They're meant to be linebackers. They tackle people. They tackle problems and issues. Sometimes when you get tackled, it hurts. But hurting you wasn't their intent. They were trying to get a job done and make something happen. They're trying to be clear and stand up for what's good, right, and true. Even when the way they said something hurt your feelings, tell them, "I want to know your heart. I want to understand you. I want to understand that what you're trying to say is for my own good, and that you're trying to speak up for what's good, right, and true."

Eights are not always as tactful as you would be. They are direct. We need people to be direct and clear in our society today. Many people tell us what we want to hear, but Eights tell us what we need to hear. If it weren't for Nathan, David wouldn't have repented. David confessed his sins and thanked God. He got his life right with God because of Nathan's confrontation. One of my favorite verses in the Bible is Psalm 51:4. In this verse, David said to the Lord, "Against you, and you alone, have I sinned." In this psalm, David talked about being cleansed from his sin, and he asked God to renew a right spirit within him. This is one of the most beautiful passages in the Bible. David's heart was exposed because David's sin was confronted. So this is the beautiful role of the Eight. Eights speak truth when no one else will.

So let's love our Eights. Let's thank God for the Challengers in our lives because we need to be challenged. If we're not challenged, we won't grow.

A Prayer for Eights

If you're an Eight, here is a prayer to pray:

God, help me to rely on You and not just my instincts. Help me find strong people who will be direct with me, but also see my heart and my intentions. God, help me show my weaknesses and experience the true strength that comes from You.

And here is my prayer for you:

Heavenly Father, I'm so grateful for the Eights who are in our lives. These strong men and women speak up for the truth, stand for what is right, and want to see justice in an unjust world. We are thankful for them. We pray that as they have a passion for justice, they would have a passion for tenderness and mercy. Give them humility, Lord, to go along with their incredible strength. We're so thankful for the Eights in our lives. Bless them, and bring more of them to us because they protect us when we cannot be strong for ourselves. We pray this in Jesus' name, amen.

THE PEACEMAKER

Peace vs. Laziness

The reason we are talking about the Nines last is that we knew they would not start a fight if we made them wait. I want to inspire all the Nines to be all that God has called you to be.

Nines in the Bible: Abraham

In this chapter, we are going to look at an incredible peacemaker in the Bible. It is interesting that when God started our faith, He chose a Nine to begin with. He chose somebody who had a heart for peacemaking and who was able to see both sides. It takes an extraordinary person to negotiate peace with God, and that is where our story begins.

Genesis 18:20 says, "So the LORD told Abraham, 'I have heard a great outcry from Sodom and Gomorrah, because their sin is so flagrant.'"

Sodom and Gomorrah are two of the most famous cities in the history of the world for all the wrong reasons. They did everything wrong and were terrible sinners. Things in Sodom and Gomorrah were so bad that it got the attention of God in heaven, and He came down to take a look to see if it was as bad as he had heard. God preemptively looked at the city to see if He was going to strike it and destroy it. Ultimately, He did. However, to check things out first, He sent down three angels as his representatives.

In verse 21, God said, "I am going to go down and see if their actions are as wicked as I have heard. If not, I want to know." God was getting all these reports about Sodom and Gomorrah. He said, *"I want to see what is happening on earth."*

"The other men turned and headed toward Sodom, but the LORD remained with Abraham" (v. 22). Not long ago, there was a classic peace summit between the United States and North Korea. There was a lot of tension revolving around nuclear war or peace. This was basically what happened in Genesis. God was going to bring down nuclear war on Sodom and Gomorrah, but Abraham interceded. Abraham tried to talk God out of destroying the most wicked cities on the wicked planet called Earth.

Here is where the story includes a classic Nine. "Abraham approached [God] and said, 'Will you sweep away both the righteous and the wicked?'" (v. 23). Abraham was saying, *"God, are You going to kill everybody in Sodom? I mean, surely not everybody there is wicked."* Then Abraham said to the Lord, "Suppose you find fifty righteous people living there in the city—will you still sweep it away and not spare it for their sakes?" (v. 24).

We do not know exactly how many people lived in Sodom

because it was ultimately destroyed. However, we know it was a massive city. It was two cities joined together. We are talking about thousands and thousands of people.

Abraham was saying to God, *"Are You going to kill everybody? I mean, surely they are not all bad apples."* He continued, "Surely you wouldn't do such a thing, destroying the righteous along with the wicked. Why, you would be treating the righteous and the wicked exactly the same! Surely you wouldn't do that! Should not the Judge of all the earth do what is right?" (v. 25). Here, Abraham was challenging the goodness of God. He was arguing, *"Not everybody can be bad."* He was trying to negotiate a peace treaty between the almighty God and the wicked city of Sodom.

What was amazing was God said, "If I find fifty righteous people living in Sodom, I will spare the entire city for their sake" (v. 26). So if there were just fifty good apples among all the rotten ones, God would not judge them. The problem was that Sodom was pretty bad.

Abraham knew this, so he kept going. Let's look at his conversation with the Lord:

> Then Abraham spoke again. "Since I have begun, let me speak further to my Lord, even though I am but dust and ashes. Suppose there are only forty-five righteous people rather than fifty? Will you destroy the whole city for lack of five?"
>
> And the LORD said, "I will not destroy it if I find forty-five righteous people there."
>
> Then Abraham pressed his request further. "Suppose there are only forty?"
>
> And the LORD replied, "I will not destroy it for the sake of the forty."

"Please don't be angry, my Lord," Abraham pleaded. "Let me speak—suppose only thirty righteous people are found?"

And the LORD replied, "I will not destroy it if I find thirty."

Then Abraham said, "Since I have dared to speak to the Lord, let me continue—suppose there are only twenty?"

And the LORD replied, "Then I will not destroy it for the sake of the twenty."

Finally, Abraham said, "Lord, please don't be angry with me if I speak one more time. Suppose only ten are found there?"

And the LORD replied, "Then I will not destroy it for the sake of the ten."

When the LORD had finished his conversation with Abraham, he went on his way, and Abraham returned to his tent. (vv. 27–33)

We know from the Bible that there were not ten righteous people in this city. It reminds us that we must be very careful about the environment and the people we surround ourselves with. A lot of people say, "I am going to be a witness to the unrighteous. I am going to be a good person in the bad bunch." The Bible says, "Don't be fooled by those who say such things, for 'bad company corrupts good character'" (1 Corinthians 15:33).

The reality was, everybody was bad in Sodom and Gomorrah. There were not even ten righteous people in the entire city. That means 99.999 percent of everybody in that entire city was evil. It was so bad that the Lord sent His messengers to the city to see it for themselves. The Bible says that all the men in Sodom, young and old, tried to rape the angels (Genesis 19:4–5). That is how bad it was. All the men of the city came out to assault God's angels.

However, Abraham was trying to negotiate peace by finding a

position where he could avoid the conflict. From Abraham's point of view, God's will is always no war. A lot of people say, "War is never the answer." My response is, "Well, what is the question?" Sometimes war is the answer. Now, we need to avoid it at all costs, but sometimes even God demands war.

The Character of Nines: They Reflect God's Peace

Nines reflect God's peace.

As you know by now, my wife and I have taken the Enneagram assessment. My wife's score is almost nonexistent for Nine, and I have to pretend I have some Nine so that there is at least some peace in our household. Tammy and I scored very low on both Five and Nine, so we do not withhold any thoughts, and we share everything that comes to mind. I have had to manufacture some Nine in my life to try to negotiate in our conflicts throughout marriage, because if no one seeks peace, someone seeks a divorce. Be thankful for Nines in your relationships.

The Core Motivation of Nines: Peace

The basic desire of Nines is to avoid conflict and create a healthy space for people to thrive. Nines are peacemakers. They want everybody to get along. They want everybody to be okay. They want to create a healthy space where you can be you and all that God has created you to be. They are wonderful, beautiful, and amazing people. This is why God chose Abraham to begin His work.

When Nines are healthy, they see multiple sides to any given decision or scenario. If you are raising a child who is a Nine, he or she will say, "Well, I hear what you are saying, Mom or Dad, but have you thought about this?" Nines are the least judgmental personality type. They can always find some good in somebody's situation. Think about Abraham: he was able to find good in the wickedest city of all time. Abraham said, "*Lord, maybe You, God almighty, omniscient, all-powerful, and all-knowing, can overlook ten people.*" God said, "*If there are even ten righteous people, I will not destroy the city.*"

So healthy Nines can see a situation from multiple angles. The Nines are right next to the Eights, but they are very different. Eights see their way or the highway. Nines see multiple routes that all lead to the same place.

Nines are inclusive and a great part of a team. Healthy Nines are fantastic as ministers and staff members. They want everybody to get the credit. They are not all about themselves, but about moving the ball forward together. They are inclusive, and they will not be exclusive to anybody. They want to make sure that everybody feels valued and gets an opportunity to contribute.

Nines are patient and accepting of others. Nines are great parents because when the rest of us are close to losing it with our two-year-olds, they say, "Well, they are learning to find themselves and testing their boundaries."

The rest of us are saying, "No, that kid needs a spanking."

However, the Nines say, "Let's give it a little time, sit back, and see what God does." Nines are so patient with the rest of us. Where the Eight has very little patience, the Nine has an overflow of patience for people. Abraham knew how evil the city of Sodom was. However, he thought that if they could just give it a chance, it would get better.

The next thing about Nines is they are good listeners. If you want to sit down and be heard, find a Nine. They care about your heart and your feelings, and they love your story. Being a good listener is one of their gifts. I am a Three, and I have a hard time listening because I know what we need to do and where we need to go right now. But Nines want to hear your story and come alongside you. They make great friends. So when you are hurt or upset and you want to share your feelings, Nines are there to listen. Nines are also great mediators. Abraham was a mediator. This is similar to how Christ is our mediator (1 Timothy 2:5). Nines try to bring two conflicting situations together. They can see where two parties are polarized, and they can get them to agree on common ground. Nines make great marriage counselors or mediators for court. If you have a child who is a Nine, and there are multiple children in your home, your Nine is always negotiating the peace.

Nines are considerate of the perspective of others. In the previous chapter, we talked about how Eights do not see your perspective and do not necessarily care about your view because they believe theirs is the right one. Nines may not agree with you, but they care about your viewpoint. They realize they could learn something if they see it from your point of view. They care about your contribution to the team, and they make sure that you have room to be heard.

Nines desire to see the world as a more peaceful place. We need peace in our lives. Nines play an important role not only in the world, but in the church. The church is full of conflict, and we need Nines to bring us together to remind us of our common purpose and our common Lord. Maybe you are ready to quit your job, or you are just fed up with your life. Nines can help you see the other side. They can help you see something you are missing.

Nines are great people to bounce things off of. If you are trying to decide between A and B, and you are not sure, the Nine can help you come up with a list of pros and cons for each option.

Unhealthy Nines do not declare their own needs. This can be really frustrating. For example, when you ask Nines where they want to go out to eat, the Nines will say they do not care, but they really do care. If you are not careful, they can become upset with you because you never ask where they want to go. Nines appreciate when you ask what their thoughts and needs are. When we have a staff meeting at Sandals Church, the Nines just sit there. Sometimes the Nines have the best decision or the best ideas, but they won't declare them. They won't state their ideas. The Eights tell me what we should do. The Threes tell me how they are right. The Sevens are in a hurry to get done with the decision so we can go have fun. Sometimes the Eights are right. However, great ideas often come from the Nines—that is, if we take the time to listen to them.

People who are married to Nines need to ask them how they are really feeling, and if those thoughts are really theirs. You need to create a safe place because they will not just tell you. They want you to read their minds. They want you to just know them and understand how to react to them. Since they will not declare their thoughts, it can create conflict because nobody knows how they feel until they share it.

When Nines do not declare their own needs, they become passive-aggressive. Nines are never going to punch you in the face. They are going to retaliate in passive-aggressive ways. For example, they may use the Internet, a story, or some other way. When they are unhealthy, Nines are going to strike when nobody's looking. If you are an Eight and are married to a Nine, you are probably dominating, and the Nine is just going along for the ride. But sooner or later, the Nine is going to be upset and strike back. Here is what can happen if you are a Nine who does not share: You may decide that you are just done with a situation because you have never declared your thoughts or feelings. By the time you get to the place where you cannot withhold it anymore, the relationship is so broken that there is no hope. Nines need to focus on declaring how they feel. Often, Nines don't share what they want because they feel it will lead to conflict.

When unhealthy, Nines can become stubborn. The Nine is similar to an elephant. When elephants are motivated, they are powerful. Similarly, when Nines are healthy, they can do great things. They can move obstacles that you never thought could be moved. One thing about elephants, though, is if they do not want to move, they will not move. Here is the thing with Nines: they can be powerful at going nowhere. If Nines are unhealthy, they will say things like, "Yep, I will do that. I will go there. We can do that." Then they will just not go, not do it. You become frustrated because you do not understand. Nines lie, but not because they are actually liars. They lie because they do not want conflict. So they tell you what you want to hear. However, you can always tell what Nines really think about by what they are doing. For Nines, action (or should I say *inaction?*) speaks much louder than words.

The Core Sin of Nines: Laziness

The Nine's core sin is laziness. An unhealthy Nine can sit forever, and he or she can outlast you. A good friend of mine, who is a super-talented Nine, says while he is working, "Why stand when you can sit? Why sit when you could lie down?" Like elephants that do not want to move, Nines will not be budged. You can try to get behind them and push them or tug them. However, even if you use all your power, they will not move. Some people may be offended by that, but if you are not offended by the core sin, it is not yours. If it does not rub you the wrong way, it is not your sin. When all these sins are mentioned and they apply to you, you do not like it.

Again, the core sin of a Nine is laziness. But Nines can be productive. They can exercise and eat well, so you might not see where laziness shows up in their lives. Some Nines turn into couch potatoes. You do not exercise, you do not take care of your body, and you do not have a high drive. Nines' best days are doing nothing. A Nine is like Jim Gaffigan, one of my favorite comics (who is clearly a Nine). He has made a lot of money doing nothing but being funny about not wanting to do anything.

Here are some points that may help you to identify how laziness affects your life. The core sin of laziness is manifested through indecision. This involves thinking, *I don't know what I should do, so I'm not going to do anything.* Indecision can lead to paralysis. This is what happens to Nines. They do not know what to do, so they don't do anything. For example, a Nine will say things like, "I do not know what I should do for a career, so I will not have a career." "I do not know what major I should pick in college, so I will not graduate from college." "I do not know who I should date, so I will not date." That is what can happen to Nines who stop and do nothing. They are like sitting elephants.

Next, laziness in Nines can show up as inaction. They know what they should do, but they do not do it. Nines can often have a list of ten things they need to do, but instead they decide they are not going to do them. If you are a Nine, this is how it can manifest in your own life: If somebody tells you that you should eat better, you respond with a criticism like, "Well, you should work out, but you don't." Or you respond with what they should do. Nines can end up not taking action on what they should do, which leads to laziness.

Next, laziness in Nines can be manifested as procrastination. Now, all of us probably procrastinate a little bit, but the Nines are great at it. They will come up with a thousand things they need to do to avoid doing what they know they should do. That's how laziness is. Laziness is not always doing nothing—it usually is about doing anything *but* what you're supposed to be doing! You're going to do all kinds of other things to avoid the one thing. For example, if a Nine has a term paper due, that person is going to clean his or her dorm room or maybe talk to a friend that he or she never talks to instead. Nines are going to do all kinds of things to avoid the one thing they're supposed to be doing.

The core sin of laziness is not doing the important or necessary things required for growth. Relationships are hard. You have to work through them, which requires growth. Another example is studying your Bible. It's hard, but that's what it takes to grow. There are all kinds of things you need to do to grow, but Nines tend to not do them. Often, they will focus on what they want. However, what they want is not always healthy.

Nines Avoid Conflict

When Nines become unhealthy, there is a huge shift. When healthy, Nines are great friends, mediators, and peacemakers. However, when they are unhealthy, Nines will avoid conflict at all costs.

This can be a problem because sometimes people need to be confronted. For example, you wouldn't be able to negotiate peace with Adolf Hitler. The world tried. When they did that, millions of people died. Sometimes there are situations where you cannot avoid conflict. You can pray and work for peace, but there may still be conflict. You may have to confront someone or something. You cannot just pray that it goes away.

Again, unhealthy Nines will avoid conflict at all costs. They typically do not commit sins by doing something. More often, their sin is not doing something. They do not get involved, and instead walk away. Because Nines avoid conflict, there can be serious consequences. Somebody may even get beat up or hurt. There are two types of sins in the Bible: sins of commission, which are things we do, and sins of omission, which are things we do not do. Nines often believe falsely that they are good people because they have not done anything wrong. When you stand before God on the day of judgment, you are going to be held accountable not only for what you did but also for what you did not do. In the parable of the talents in Matthew 25:14–28, three people have talents, or units of money. One person has five, another person has two, and the last person is only given one talent. The person with only one is judged because he buried his talent in the ground and did nothing with it. The master said to him, "You wicked and lazy servant!" (v. 26). You need to know that we are called to do things. We cannot just live our lives avoiding everything. Nines have to remember to engage and be active. Nines, remember that God will not hold you accountable for the gifts you don't have, but He does expect you to actively use the gifts and talents you do have.

The beauty of healthy Nines is they are always in pursuit of embracing conflict. They are never going to love it, and that's okay. I don't particularly love conflict either. I'm not high enough as an Eight for that. However, I sometimes have to embrace conflict.

Sometimes you have to have a conflict to work things out. A lot of Nines will say that they never have conflict in their marriage. They never fight about anything. Then all of a sudden, fifteen to twenty years later, they'll say, "We just grew apart." Well, the reason they grew apart is because they were never willing to engage and have the tough conversations to declare what they like or how they feel. A healthy Nine is in pursuit of embracing healthy conflict. If you are a Nine, you probably think, *I don't want to do this because it's going to lead to a fight.* However, what you should be asking yourself is, *Even though it is going to lead to conflict, will it lead to a positive outcome?*

Nines have to declare their wants and their needs as a means of deeper connection with themselves and others. People can't love you if they don't know you. The primary way we get to know people is by declaring things. For example, "Here's what I think, here's how I feel, and here's what I want." If you have multiple kids and one of them is a Nine, he or she will probably never say what his or her favorite ice cream is. He or she is just going to eat what everybody else wants. Nines are going to do what everybody else does. That's not good for life because God created you as an individual. You have your own likes, dislikes, needs, wants, and desires. You've got to learn to declare them because Nines can just slip in with other people and never be who God has called them to be. Healthy Nines are always in pursuit of embracing conflict and declaring their wants and needs as a means of deeper connection.

Let's talk about that in regard to Abraham. Abraham was a great peacemaker. This was not always a good thing. Abraham had two wives. Sarah was his first wife. Eventually, he took Hagar, a servant, on as a concubine. In Genesis 16, Hagar got pregnant with Abraham's son and named him Ishmael. This caused a conflict between Sarah and Hagar. So Sarah told Abraham that she wanted him to get rid of Hagar and Ishmael. Now, here's what a healthy Nine would do. He would say, "Sarah, I can understand why you want me to do this, but you're the one who asked me to have a child with Hagar." Unhealthy Nines are not going to do that. They're not going to be declarative. Abraham didn't tell Sarah that he really cared for his son, Ishmael. He didn't say how much Ishmael mattered to him and that he loved him deeply. He never declared his needs. So in order to maintain the peace in his home, he effectively sentenced Hagar and Ishmael to death by sending them away (although they didn't die—God had to step in for them). He did this because he couldn't declare his own needs.

Another time, in Genesis 13, Abraham had conflict with his nephew, Lot. Lot wasn't entitled to any money, influence, or power underneath Abraham's leadership. However, Lot ended up growing in wealth and power. Lot grew in all kinds of ways, but he was constantly in trouble. So their herdsmen started fighting, and there was conflict. Abraham said, "*I don't want to fight. I want you to choose. If you choose the left, I'll choose the right. If you choose the right, I'll choose the left. Wherever you go, I won't go.*" Ultimately, that led to the doom of Lot and his family. Abraham failed to confront his spoiled nephew and say, "*Lot, I've given you everything you have, and you're a spoiled brat. Now it's time to listen to me.*" He didn't do that. Since Abraham failed to confront Lot, Lot was cursed for generations. This happened in part because Lot didn't have an uncle who spoke truth into his life.

If you're a Nine, you're probably not going to want to speak into your family member's life. You're not going to want to confront your sons or your daughters because you don't want to cause conflict. You don't want to ruffle the feathers. However, if you don't do this, you will be creating a disaster for the future of the people you love. It's not easy to confront your kids, but you need to because you need to raise your kids to choose what is good, moral, right, and true. This isn't going to happen if you sit back and say, "Well, it's up to God." God has placed you in charge, and you have to step in to say, "You blew it." Tell your child, "I wish we could just have fun and have a good time. However, this has to be addressed first." Tell your child, "I don't want to have this conversation, but you are screwing up."

Abraham's intent as a Nine was not to harm Hagar and Ishmael. It wasn't to harm Lot, his wife, and their kids. However, ultimately, Abraham's desire for peace trumped his desire for what was good, right, and true. Nines have to talk about what's moral, good, right, and true over what's peaceful, because peace is not always the best thing. This is true, especially, when it negatively affects the people God loves. That includes you, your family, your friends, and most important, your church. So, again, Nines have to be declarative.

How Nines Can Be Real with Self, Others, and God

How can Nines learn how to be real with themselves, with others, and with God?

Real with Self

Nines need to own and resolve their own feelings. This is a big, big deal. The thing about Nines is that they are so good at listening to everybody else's soul, they forget they have a soul. They're so good at listening to everybody else's feelings that they forget their own feelings. The reason Nines don't declare how they feel is because they're too busy trying to maintain peace between everybody else. They're not thinking about their own feelings and thoughts. They're trying to resolve everybody else's feelings, and they negate their own. So Nines have to own and resolve their own emotions.

Real with Others

People can't know you and love you until you own and declare your feelings to them. You have to say things like, "Here's how I feel" and "Here's what I'm thinking." "This really made me upset" and "This really hurt my feelings." If you're a Nine and you're married to someone who's not a Nine, you have to tell your spouse that declaring your feelings is really hard for you. Even though it is difficult and you don't want to do it, you know it is for the best.

Not only do you have to own your needs and feelings, but you also have to make declarative statements: "I don't like that." "I don't agree." "I think we should go left and not right." "I think you're wrong." "I think he's right." Declarative statements are statements that are clear. They're not wishy-washy, and they don't say that you can see both sides. It's making a statement that lets everybody else understand which side you're on. You either agree or you disagree. You can't leave any gray area. Nines live in the gray areas, which drives people crazy. So just say what you feel and think as a Christian, child of God, and mature adult. Embrace that conflict isn't necessarily always bad, and your involvement can lead to the resolution.

Here's why we need Nines involved: they're going to help bring about peace. But they can't bring peace by pretending there's not a conflict. So when conversations in a small group get awkward or heated, that's when the Nines need to be active. Typically, what you do as a Nine is go hide in your shell. You act like you're a turtle, and you just disappear until the smoke clears. When you come out, that's when you need to be involved. We don't want the Eights or Threes to resolve it. We want the Nines to speak and be declarative to help bring healing to the group. The problem is that the people we need to speak up the most speak up the least. That's a huge challenge.

Real with God

In order to be real with God, Nines have to pursue faith with action. People might not want to be honest with you about this, but laziness is a real thing and it's a sin. If you're a Nine, chances are laziness affects you. Maybe God gave you a slow motor, and that's fine, but be an elephant. When you move, you have to be powerful and pursue faith with action. You have to do something. God doesn't just want you to think, reflect, or be a yoga instructor. Nines are super spiritual and often they can mask their inaction with spiritual language. So it can feel like they're doing something when they're actually not doing anything.

Nines, you can think something, feel something, and believe something, but you need to do something. So, again, pursue faith with action. The Bible says this in Romans 12:11: "Never be lazy, but work hard and serve the Lord enthusiastically." Nines, use your gifts for the glory of God. You don't have to be a sprinter, but you do need to move. You need to move for God, and you need to work for God. You can't just sit back and let everybody else do it. You have to make sure that you are serving God.

How Do You Love a Nine?

If you have Nines in your life, let me give you some helpful hints for how to love them and care for them.

1. Create an environment where their voices are heard and matter.

Nines are not going to want to speak up. If they do speak up and you shut them down, guess what will happen? They will never be honest with you ever again. So be sure to create an environment where they feel that their opinion matters.

When we're having a staff meeting, and I know there are Nines present, I'll say, "We've heard from everyone else. Nines, I need you to speak up." Just so I don't make them panic, I say at the outset, "Hey, guys. I know the Nines aren't going to share anything, so at the end of the meeting, I'm going to ask the Nines to make declarative statements about what they thought." That may freak them out, but I want to hear from the Nines because the Threes, Eights, and Sevens have more boisterous personalities. They'll take control. We need to hear the Nines to make sure we don't miss something.

If you have several kids and one of them is a Nine, you have to make the other kids stop and listen. They need to show respect while the Nine in the family speaks up, because Nines matter. We care about Nines and want to create an environment where their voices are heard. If you're a Nine and you grew up in a home where your voice didn't matter or it was squashed when you spoke up, I'm sorry that happened. We need to come alongside you to help you grow and to create environments where you are heard. I know personalities like mine can be overwhelming. We tend to squelch other ideas, and I apologize for that. You do matter to God and to us.

2. Don't shield them from all conflict.

If you're married to a Nine, you can block all conflict from them, but you're not doing them a favor. There is conflict in life, and conflict brings growth. So if you're constantly blocking your spouse or your child from every single difficult thing, you're not helping them. You're actually hurting them. Just like Abraham hurt Lot. Eventually, guess what happened? Lot's wife died, and his life was a disaster. Abraham should have spoken the truth to Lot and not blocked conflict. He should have just said, "Your people are just as responsible as my people for this conflict. Let's sit down and figure out a solution that doesn't involve breaking up the family." Unfortunately, that was not the solution they came to. So don't shield Nines from conflict; instead, encourage them to actively engage.

3. Celebrate with them when they finish projects.

It's very difficult for Nines to finish projects. They will be working on fifty things and finishing zero things. So when they finish a term paper, a dissertation, a job, a project, or something you've asked them to do, you need to celebrate that. It's not unlike Nines to say, "I'm going to get to it" over and over. Then they never do get to it. This doesn't mean they're lying. They have the intent to get to it, and they believe they are going to. But there are so many other things in the way. So celebrate with them when they finish something. Make a big deal of it. Don't put them down and say, "Well, it's about time you finished something." Celebrate them and encourage them. Human beings love to be rewarded when they do good things. Nines do also, so tell them what they finished is great. If you raise a child who is a Nine, he or she is probably not going to want to finish the baseball season or the soccer season. Don't make your child sign up again. Celebrate when he or she survives a season or gets through a difficult situation. This is really, really important, because people who can't finish projects don't finish life well. So we need to encourage them.

4. Don't push them to sprint.

For example, when raising Nines, maybe the track team isn't for them. It may not be the best sport to involve them in. That's not to say that Nines don't need to be active. We told our kids that we want them to do something active because we're not raising couch potatoes. We're raising kids for Christ. So you have to pick something for them to do. I told my kids, "Either you pick or I pick." A couple of my kids didn't pick, so we picked. Pick something for your kids to do, but don't push your Nines to be sprinters, especially if you're a Three. I'm a Three. Remember—I did an Ironman during my time off. Nines are probably not going to do that. They find watching an Ironman exhausting. So if you're married to a Nine and you want to run together, agree to walk together. If you run at a different pace, that's going to create conflict. That's fine. Remember the old story about the tortoise and the hare? The hare sprints, but the tortoise goes slow. The tortoise does finish the race, eventually. He actually passes the hare and wins because the hare is so overly confident that he takes a nap in the middle of the race. So just know that we have to encourage the Nines in our lives, who are like the tortoise.

5. Thank them for their gift of seeing the other side of things.

I cannot tell you how much we need that wisdom in our world. Think about the racial issues in our country—the racial divide. Nines are great at seeing the perspective of both blacks and whites and bringing us together. They are also great at seeing the perspective of men and women, parents and kids, and Republicans and Democrats. This is a skill our world needs, so we need to thank Nines for their ability to see multiple sides of the same thing. A lot of us only see in black and white. Nines can see the gray.

Nines, I love you, and I care for you. I want you to be declarative, and I want you to get some things done in life. God has called you. There's a reason God chose Abraham—because Abraham could get things done. But when you read his story, you'll see he kind of gets stuck at certain places. He has a hard time being declarative. Just know that your laziness and not being declarative can be terrible for the people you love. I want you to be able to be declarative, truthful, and clear about what it is that God's calling you to do.

A Prayer for Nines

Here's a prayer for Nines to pray.

Lord, help me to share my thoughts and feelings in healthy ways. Empower me to engage in conflict and have tough conversations when it's necessary for growth.

This is my prayer for you.

God, thank You for our Nines. They help bring peace to our lives when all there seems to be around us is war. Lord, help them to find the voice You gave them—a voice full of wisdom and perspective. Help them use that voice to help the rest of us see the other side. Lord, as they see us, help them to see themselves. As they see our conflicts, help them see their internal conflict. Jesus, our Peace King, as You were never afraid to declare truth, help Nines rise with Your power and strength to declare what is good and right and true! In Jesus' name we pray, amen.

CONCLUSION

What's My Number?

Many people feel so much anxiety and stress over discovering their Enneagram number. As you have discovered in this book, I mostly identify as a Three. But I also wrestle with my emotions, showing that I also have a strong Four gifting. And because I like to have too much fun, I also score as a high Seven. I also hate to be controlled, which points out the high Eight in me. All these numbers play into who I am. If you have finished this book and are still confused, these questions might help.

1. Did you feel angry as you read through my chapters and notice areas where I spent too much time on the gifting of one personality and glanced over the weakness and struggles of another? Should I have addressed your spouse's big issue? You're probably a One.

2. Were you thankful you didn't identify with any of the numbers? Did you take meticulous notes on the weakness of all the numbers and can't wait to "help" people with their presently unidentified weaknesses? Especially those who can't see their sin because of pride? You are probably a Two.

3. Are you thrilled that you have become an Enneagram expert and can't wait to amaze and dazzle your friends with your newfound knowledge? Could some of my stories, with just a mild amount of tweaking, have been yours? You are definitely a Three.

4. Does the entire numbers thing make you feel ordinary? Do you feel that no book could ever describe the depth of who you are? But at the same time, do you find something in each personality type that you wish you had? There's a good chance you are a Four . . . although no number can contain you.

5. Did you write your own book within the margins of this book or in the notes feature of your eBook reader? Or did it take you twice as long to listen to the audio because you kept stopping to fill up a journal? Have you downloaded every book you can find and researched all information on the Enneagram? Are you crafting a deeply thought-provoking and accurate account of where the Enneagram really came from? But you might never press Send? You're a Five!

6. As we went through the core sin and struggle of each personality type, were you afraid you had all the bad traits and none of the good ones? Have you taken numerous tests that all point to you being a Six, but you can't trust the results because you took the test? You're a probably a Six.

7. Did reading this book make you feel boxed in or trapped? Did you stop reading and instantly watch *Footloose*, both the original Kevin Bacon version and the newer one? Are you ready to stop reading and start living? You're probably a Seven.

8. This is all ridiculous! Psychobabble! No book can read you. Enneagram, schmemeagram. No question—you're an Eight! Deal with it . . . since we have to!

9. Do you need a nap? Did this book arouse unwanted conflict? Did you pick up this book, lose this book, find this book? Have you yet to finish this book? You're probably a Nine.

Look, here is the good news. You're not just a number. You were made in the image of God. The Bible teaches that before the foundation of the world was laid, God knew you. You and I have no idea when "before the world began" was, but the Fives will soon have a chart or graph that explains it, and the Ones will add corrections to improve it later! Before the Enneagram was even a thing, God knew you. And He loved you so much that He sent His Son to die for you on the cross.

The Enneagram can begin to help you unpack yourself and see what God made. It can help you see the good in you that needs to be blessed, the bad in you that needs to be changed, and the brokenness in you that needs to be healed. But the Enneagram, despite all its wonders, is not Jesus. It is full of wisdom, but it is not full of God's Spirit. It can help your life, but it cannot provide new life. The Enneagram can only help, but it cannot heal. In the fifth chapter of the gospel of John, we see Jesus at the pool of Bethesda. This pool was thought to be a place of healing, but I imagine it smelled like a giant porta-potty! Think about all these people who are sick . . . ever been to the emergency room? If you weren't sick when you went in, you probably were when you went out! Around this pool packed with sick people, the surface is covered in human waste and vomit. So why would people do it—why would they go? Smells and fluids are of no consequence if you feel like you are dying! Besides, two thousand years ago medicine was in its infancy, and doctors (if you could even call them that) usually did much more harm than good. So the poop pool it is.

The story states that around this crowed pool, one man who had been ill for thirty-eight years lay beside the pool every day, believing it would heal him. Baths help, but Jesus heals. Jesus asked the man a very serious question. *"Do you want to get well?"* His response is incredible: *"I have no one to help me."* I would have said, "Of course!" But I know Jesus. This man may not have. This man may be like you. Maybe you have rejected Jesus because you have never met Jesus! I meet many people who reject Jesus for all kinds of reasons. Usually their rejection of Jesus has nothing to do with Jesus but because they misunderstand who He is.

Oftentimes people reject Jesus because of someone who claims to know Him! People claim to know me all the time. People say they have known me for years. Sometimes people put me down as their job reference, and I have to tell the employer who is calling, "I have no idea who this person is." Just because somebody claims to know Jesus doesn't mean He knows them. As a matter of fact, Jesus specifically stated in Matthew 7 that there will be many people who claim to know Him, but He will say, *"I never knew them."* These people could even be pastors or a powerful church member. Or just someone with an I LOVE JESUS shirt or a WWJD bracelet. Just because they claim Him doesn't mean they know Him.

This book isn't about them—it's about YOU! Jesus—the real

Jesus!—said, *"Do you want to get well?"* The question demanded a yes-or-no answer—but the man at the pool of Bethesda said neither. Instead, he talked about others who did not help him. If you were not careful when reading this book, maybe you identified every unhealthy person in your life who didn't help you. Instead of assessing your own life, you became a self-identified expert on others. But this book's title doesn't focus on THEM! It's a book about YOU, and Jesus is asking you, "Do you want to get well?"

I hope the Enneagram helps you. I hope this book has encouraged you. But Jesus wants to heal you. *Do you want to get well?* Without Jesus, the Enneagram might even make you worse. Can you imagine? In the hands a surgeon, a scalpel is a good thing, but in the hands of a child, it's a very dangerous thing. We are all children when it comes to understanding ourselves, God, and others. Unfortunately, like what happened with Eve and Adam in our opening chapter, you may have believed this new fruit would change everything for the better or that you could grow in knowledge without God. The Devil always promises life—but it never works out that way!

Jesus doesn't need healing, because He is healing. Jesus said, "[I] came to seek and save those who are lost" (Luke 19:10). That's you! That's me! Has Jesus saved you? Jesus told the man at the pool to get up, pick up his sleeping mat, and walk. And the man did. The same Spirit of God who hovered over the darkness of the earth when it was formless and void is hovering over the darkest parts of your life. The God of the universe wants to heal you, to make you whole. The Enneagram can only help you understand what's wrong. Jesus and Jesus alone can make all things right, because He makes all things new. If you want to be healed, all you need to do are these three things:

1. Get Real with Yourself

The Bible teaches that we are all sinners. Look, as a Three, I have to confess I can't even live up to my own standards, much less God's. The Bible says that to be saved by Jesus, I must repent of my sin. In each chapter of this book, we identified the core sin of each personality type. Have you ever repented of your sin to God? Repenting is completely changing, turning from self to God. Are you ready to change? From the standpoint of heaven, healing starts with a desire to change. Jesus will only change you if you let Him. Repenting is simply saying to God, "I am ready to change. I am ready to turn from my sin and turn to You!"

2. Get Real with God

To truly change, we all need help, but only Jesus can help you. Jesus is known by Christians as the God-man. He was fully God and became fully man when He was born in Bethlehem. He had to be both if He was going to bring mankind and God back together. Jesus died so you could live. Not your same old life but a new and awesome life. But for you to experience this, you must believe that Jesus died in your place for your sin. And here is the best part of the good news: He didn't just die; He rose from the dead! Look it up, Fives! Fact check me, Ones! This isn't fake news—it's the best news ever.

When you believe in Jesus, not only are your sins forgiven, but your soul is going to live with Him forever. Not only did Jesus die, but by faith you died with Him. The old is past and the new has begun. And the most important thing about you will not be your Enneagram number but that you are numbered as a follower of Jesus. And as a follower of Jesus, you can discover your true self, your real self. The self you were meant to be. The self God knows you can be!

Become Real with Others

You can never fully discover who you are on you own. You cannot find yourself by hiding from others! Just like in the garden of Eden when Adam and Eve covered themselves from each other as they hid from God. Now that God has found you, it's time to stop hiding from others. It's time to get real! Find a local group of believers you can be real with. They are everywhere. Authenticity is scary, but it's so worth it!

Thank you so much for reading *A Book Called YOU*. Jesus Christ has used the Enneagram to show me His continual work of healing in my life. May the Healer use this book to touch you and change your life forever.

NOTES

Introduction: Why You?
1. Rick Warren, *The Purpose Driven Life* (Grand Rapids, MI: Zondervan, 2002), 17.

Chapter 3: The Achiever
1. "The Wright Brothers: The Aerial Age Begins: 1908," Smithsonian National Air and Space Museum, https://airandspace.si.edu /exhibitions/wright-brothers/online/age/1908/index.cfm.

Chapter 5: The Observer
1. Chuck Squatriglia, "'Sully' Calmly Announced 'We're Gonna Be in the Hudson,'" *Wired*, February 5, 2009, https://www.wired.com /2009/02/sully-calmly-to/.

Chapter 8: The Challenger
1. "We Shall Fight on the Beaches" (speech), International Churchill Society, June 4, 1940, https://winstonchurchill.org/resources /speeches/1940-the-finest-hour/we-shall-fight-on-the-beaches/.
2. Peter Burrows and Ronald Glover, with Heather Green, "Steve Jobs' Magic Kingdom, Bloomberg, February 5, 2006, https://www .bloomberg.com/news/articles/2006-02-05/steve-jobs-magic-kingdom.

ABOUT THE AUTHOR

Pastor Matt Brown is the founding and lead pastor of Sandals Church in Riverside, California. Sandals Church began in 1997, when Pastor Matt and his wife, Tammy, set out to create a church where people could be real with themselves, God, and others. From its first meeting in the Browns' living room with eight people, Sandals Church has grown to include twelve physical campuses throughout California and thirteen Sandals Church Anywhere locations across the United States, Australia, the United Kingdom, and Canada. In addition, Sandals Church has a growing online campus, with people from sixty-three countries tuning in to hear the sermon each week, as well as a podcast called *The Debrief* with Matt Brown, where Pastor Matt tackles biblical truths and cultural issues in an informative and humorous way.

Today, Pastor Matt continues to lead Sandals Church as the primary teaching pastor. And in 2019, Pastor Matt and Sandals

Church launched the ROGO Foundation, which exists to help save and replant dying churches and invest in up-and-coming leaders through hands-on leadership training programs at Sandals Church.

Pastor Matt is passionate about the vision of authenticity and raising up the next generation of leaders for the local church. He and Tammy have three children and reside in Riverside, California.